# 20 Questions That Jehovah's Witnesses Cannot Answer

## By Charles Love

Plus: Charles Love, an ex-Witness elder shares his powerful testimony and his 30 year journey from Jehovah's witnesses to Jesus.

xulon
PRESS

THIS BOOK IS DEDICATED TO
THE LOVE OF MY LIFE
MY WIFE OF OVER 40 YEARS
DEANNA.

THIS STORY COULD NOT HAVE
BEEN WRITTEN WITHOUT HER.

# Table of Contents

# 20 Questions
# That
# Jehovah's witnesses
# Cannot Answer

# CHAPTER 1

# An Introduction

My Name is Charles Love, the author of this book. I was a Jehovah's witness for 30 years. This is a story that should have been written 20 years ago. At least that is what my friends tell me. Maybe it should have. But I believe that the timing of God is always correct, and I have been waiting for Him to move me to finally get this book written.

Well, it happened and here is the finished product. I believe the Lord has given me a powerful tool that will lead many to Him and will rescue many from eternal death. It is my hope that "thinking" Jehovah's witnesses or sincere people who are thinking about joining Jehovah's witnesses might find the REAL TRUTH in this book.

This book is not about bashing Jehovah's witnesses. I love Jehovah's witnesses. I was a member for over 30 years. I never wanted to leave them.

My mother at the writing of this book is still a Jehovah's witness. My father, died, believing as a Jehovah's witness.

My wife of 40 years, Deanna, has parents that are still Jehovah's witnesses.

I was a second generation Jehovah's witness. My wife was a third generation Witness.

All of her grandparents were "of the anointed". That means they were part of the 144,000 class of Jehovah's witnesses. Later in this book, I will explain what that means.

This book is not a hate book. It is a love book to all in Jehovah's witnesses and to all who may be studying with them, and with all who will be contacted by them this week.

All I ask you to do as you read this book is to be honest. The truth is always the truth. You can investigate it a thousand times, but the truth is always the truth.

Take your Bible and challenge everything I say. If I am wrong, let me know where. I only want to promote the truth that leads to salvation. I have no other motives. I want you however, to understand this. If you have truth, you never need to be afraid to investigate what others call the truth. Truth will eventually shine forth, and the lie will eventually fall under scrutiny. Beware of those who want you to close your mind and do not want you to search out truth.

It was my experience that as the light of the Bible shined on the "truth" of Jehovah's witnesses, the real truth of the Bible came through and the "truth" of the Witnesses couldn't stand up under the light of God's word.

You will never understand that until you investigate. I welcome your response. My E-mail address can be found at the end of this book. All correspondence will be answered and also kept confidential. I realize that many Witnesses may have questions but they do not want their identity passed around. You can have full confidence that I will never share your name with anyone. I have "been there" and I know how important confidentiality is to you.

If you are a Witness, there are several powerful questions in this book that if the Jehovah's witness organization cannot answer, absolutely puts you, your family and other loved ones in danger of missing out on God's blessed salvation altogether.

That makes many of the items discussed in this book a life and death matter for you and your family. When you are dealing with religion and salvation it is important that you make the right decision.

To blindly follow anyone, or any organization without asking the tough questions about salvation and where their proof is for their doctrine is dangerous. It can lead to death and eternal separation from God.

I trust this book will be a life saving blessing to you and your family. I write it for no other reason! But let me warn you, before you read any more of this book. I talk a lot about Jesus in this book!!

If you are ready, then let's begin together!! Praise the beautiful name of Jesus!

# CHAPTER 2

# A Brief History Of
# Jehovah's witnesses

What is known today, as the religion of Jehovah's witnesses was started by Charles Taze Russell. He was born in 1852. Charles Russell was brought up as a Congregationalist. One night Russell went to an Adventist meeting, and was told that Jesus would be back at any time. This interested Russell and got him really interested in the Bible.

The big leader of Adventism had been William Miller. Miller was a powerful preacher who predicted that the world would end in 1843. When it didn't, he "discovered" an arithmetical error in his eschatological calculations and said it would end in 1844.

This arithmetical error lesson would come in handy to the organization that Russell would establish. The Jehovah's witnesses made many arithmetical errors, as they made many eschatological mess-ups throughout their long history. Every time their predictions didn't happen, somebody blamed it on the arithmetic!! I guess God doesn't have a calculator and can't count. It is obvious that neither can the faithful and discreet slave count!! I am being sarcastic. Forgive me.

In 1844, Miller's prediction again failed. Russell became frustrated and withdrew from the Adventist movement. This brief encounter with Adventism greatly influenced Charles Russell. Eventually he took the title "Pastor" even though he never got through high school. In 1879, he began the Watch Tower. Later it would be known as the Watchtower Bible and Tract Society, the teaching organ of the Jehovah's Witnesses. In 1908 Russell moved its headquarters to Brooklyn, where it remains today.

Russell taught his followers that hell was not hot and that unsaved people would simply go out of existence at their death. He also taught the non-existence of the Trinity. He said that Jesus was Michael the Archangel and his teachings reduced the Holy Spirit from a person to a force. Russell taught the mortality of the soul and he also taught that Jesus would return in 1914.

When 1914 had come and gone, with no Jesus in sight, Russell modified his teachings and claimed Jesus had, in fact, returned to Earth, but that His return was invisible. His visible return would come later, but still very soon. It would result in the final conflict between God and the Devil in which God would be victorious. Witnesses know this conflict as the battle of Armageddon, and just about everything the Witnesses teach centers around this doctrine. I personally taught that doctrine as I went door to door preaching the Witness word.

Russell died in 1916 and was succeeded by "Judge" Joseph R. Rutherford. Rutherford, "The Judge" was born in 1869. He had been brought up as a Baptist and became the legal adviser to the Watch Tower Society. He never was a real judge, but took the title because, as an attorney, he substituted at least once for an absent judge.

At one time he claimed Russell was as good as Paul as an expounder of the gospel, but later, in an effort to have his writings gain importance, he let Russell's books go out of print. It was Rutherford who coined the slogan, "Millions now living will never die."

What he meant by that statement was that some people alive in 1914 would still be alive when Armageddon came and the world was restored to a paradise state.

In 1931 Rutherford changed the name of the organization to the Jehovah's witnesses, which he based on Isaiah 43:10 ("'You are my witnesses,' is the utterance of Jehovah, 'even my servant whom I have chosen . . .'" *New World Translation*).

Rutherford was a great organizational man. He was sometimes even ahead of his time. It was Rutherford who equipped the Witnesses with portable phonographs, which they took door to door, playing records of Rutherford. This was an innovative way to spread the Witness doctrine.

As we will see later, Rutherford had a very messed up theology. As an example, Rutherford said that in 1925 Abraham, Isaac, Jacob, and the prophets would return to Earth. He prepared for them a mansion named Beth Sarim in San Diego, California.

He personally moved into this mansion and bought an automobile with which to drive the resurrected patriarchs around. The Watch Tower Society quietly sold Beth Sarim many years later to cover up an embarrassing moment in their history, namely another failed prophecy.

Nathan Homer Knorr, who was born in 1905 and died in 1977, succeeded Rutherford. As I will talk about later, I met Nathan

Knorr and had him in my home. Knorr joined the movement as a teenager, and worked his way up through the ranks. Knorr was an even better organizational man than Rutherford! He got rid of Rutherford's old phonographs and insisted that the Witnesses be trained in personal door-to-door evangelism techniques.

Because the Bible did not support the peculiar doctrines of the Witnesses, Knorr chose an anonymous committee of five Jehovah's witnesses to produce the Jehovah's witnesses Bible called *The New World Translation*, which is used today by no one else, other than the Witnesses. Four of the five members that Knorr chose to *produce The New World Translation* completely lacked credentials to qualify them as Bible translators, and the fifth member studied non-biblical Greek for only about two years.

The *New World Translation* was produced because it supported Witnesses' beliefs through inaccurate renderings. For example, to prove that Jesus was only a creature and not God, the *New World Translation's* rendering of John 1:1 concludes this way: "and the Word was *a god*" [italics added].

Every other translation, Catholic and Protestant—not to mention the Greek original—has "and the Word was God."

Frederick Franz succeeded Knorr as head of the Jehovah's witnesses. He had been the Witnesses' leading theologian, and his services were often called upon.

I can remember going to conventions of Jehovah's witnesses and listening to Franz speak. He was the theology expert for the Witnesses!! For some years the Witnesses magazines had been predicting that Armageddon would occur in 1975. When it didn't, Franz had to find an explanation. The reason the Witnesses were looking for Armageddon in 1975 is that they believe that Adam was created in 4026 B.C. and that human beings have been allotted 6000 years of existence until Armageddon and the beginning of the millennium.

This figure is based on a "creative week" in which each of six days is equal to 1,000 years, with the Sabbath or seventh day being the beginning of the millennium. Simple arithmetic gives 1975 as the year Armageddon would arrive.

Franz explained that Armageddon would actually come 6000 years after Eve's creation. But when 1975 came and went, the Witnesses had to "adjust" their chronology to cover up a failed prediction.

They accomplished this by maintaining that no one knew exactly how long after Adam's creation Eve came on the scene. Franz said that it was months, even years. By saying that he was able to "stretch" the 1975 date to some time in the future. In any case, Franz said that Witnesses would just have to wait, knowing the end is right around the corner.

Milton Henschel succeeded Franz as president of the Watchtower in 1993. In 1995 the Watchtower quietly changed one of its major prophetic doctrines. Up until 1995, the Witnesses had maintained that the generation alive in 1914 would not pass from the scene until Armageddon occurred.

Now that this generation has almost entirely died out—and Armageddon has not occurred and does not seem like it will happen immediately—they had to change their doctrine. Now, the Watchtower says that Armageddon will simply occur "soon," and it is no longer tied to a particular, literal generation of people. This was a major point that destroyed the theology they had taught for more than 70 years and the change was hardly noticed by the average Jehovah's witness.

Do we see the pattern. It goes all the way back to Russell and William Miller. The pattern is: Make a prediction and when it fails, change the arithmetic. You will see as we discover in this book, that the pattern remains today in Jehovah's witnesses!

Most religions welcome converts, and Jehovah's witnesses are no different. To help them accomplish this they follow several steps. First they try to get a copy of one of their magazines into the hands of a prospective convert. They knock on your door and ask a question, such as, "How would you like to live in a world without sickness, war, poverty, or any other problem?"

If the prospect is willing to speak with them, they arrange what is known as a "back call" or a "return visit". What that means is they will return to that person's house in a week or two for more discussions. This can be kept up indefinitely.

At some point the Witness will invite the prospect to a Bible study. This is not the usual sort of Bible study, where passages are examined in light of context, original word meaning, relevance to other verses in Scripture, etc.

Instead, this "Bible study" is really an exposition of Witness doctrine by means of Watchtower literature. Simple questions are presented in the literature, which are derived directly from the text. The answers are easily discernible, making the prospective convert feel spiritually astute, since he or she can answer all the questions "correctly."

The Bible study is directed along lines mandated by the officials in Brooklyn, and the prospect is there to learn, not to teach. If he progresses well, he's invited to attend Sunday service at the Kingdom Hall.

The Kingdom Hall, resembles not so much a church but a small lecture hall. At the Sunday service, the prospect hears a lecture for about an hour, and then the congregation studies an article found in the Watchtower. This same Watchtower study is studied the same week in all congregations.

The prospective convert gets still more of this if he proceeds to the next step, which consists of going to meetings on Tuesday, Wednesday or Thursday nights. At those meetings, Witnesses are trained how to speak. Everyone in the congregation is enrolled in what is called the ministry school. They learn to speak in front of a group and they learn how to handle objections to their faith. It is a great training program. I taught it for years in the Witnesses congregations.

As part of the process, prospects also attend a book study produced by the Watchtower Society. The books have questions at the bottom of each page or in the lesson and Witnesses robotically answer the questions, leading the prospect to further indoctrination of Witness doctrine.

Each month each Kingdom Hall mails to the headquarters in Brooklyn a detailed log of activities, including hours spent "witnessing" door-to-door, the number of converts made, and the number of pieces of literature distributed, etc.

If the prospect goes through all these steps, he's ready for admission to Jehovah's witnesses. Becoming a member of Jehovah's witnesses, involves baptism by immersion and agreeing to work actively as a Witness, spreading the gospel of Jehovah's witnesses.

Some Jehovah's witnesses decide to become missionaries. They were known as Pioneers when I was growing up. Many Pioneers take only part-time jobs so they can devote more time to their witnessing. Pioneers will typically spend 60-100 hours each month in their door-to-door work.

Some will even go so far as to work full time for the Watchtower Society at their headquarters in New York, receiving little more than room and board for their efforts.

Every Witness is expected to do what he can to spread the Witnesses doctrine. There is no separate, ordained ministry as is found in Protestant churches. Each local Witness congregation is run by Elders under the strict supervision of the Watchtower Bible and Tract Society.

The Watchtower Bible and Tract Society, operates no hospitals, sanitariums, orphanages, schools, colleges, or social welfare agencies. From their perspective it will all disappear in a few years anyway, so they don't expend their energies in these areas.

Jehovah's witnesses live under a strict regimen. They may be "disfellowshipped" for a variety of reasons, such as attending a Catholic or Protestant church or receiving a blood transfusion. I remember when my non-witness grandfather died, we could not go into the church for the service. We remained outside of the church until the service was over. How ridiculous that was!!

Disfellowshipping is the Witnesses act of excommunication. A disfellowshipped Witness may attend the Kingdom Hall, but he/she is not allowed to speak to anyone, and no one may speak to him or her, including his or her family. The others are to act as though he/she no longer exists. After a period of time, if the disfellowshipped person displays a "repentant attitude" he or she may be "reinstated" with full privileges restored.

While I was never disfellowshipped, Jehovah's witnesses will not talk to me today.

Jehovah's witnesses, recognize the legitimacy of no governmental authority, since they believe all earthly authority including that of the United States is of Satan. Jehovah's witnesses will not serve in the military, salute the flag, stand for the National Anthem, say the Pledge of Allegiance, vote, run for office, or serve as officials of labor unions. They do not celebrate any of the holidays, nor do they associate with other non-Jehovah's witnesses. Their view of non-Jehovah's witnesses is that they are all doomed and for the most part belong to Satan's crowd. They believe that they are the only true religion on earth. All other religions are destined for destruction at the battle of Armageddon. If you believe in Jesus and are Born Again, the Witnesses view you as part of the enemy!

No matter how peculiar their doctrines, they deserve to be complimented on their determination and single-minded zeal. However, as Paul might have said concerning them, "I can testify about them that they are zealous for God, but their zeal is not based on knowledge" (Rom. 10:2, NIV).

So there you have a brief history of Jehovah's witnesses.

At the writing of this book there are millions of Jehovah's witnesses. They are very active in spreading their religious teachings. We could learn a lesson from Jehovah's witnesses. We should be as zealous as they are in spreading the gospel, because it is the Christian gospel that saves. As we shall soon see, it is the Witness doctrine that enslaves.

# CHAPTER 3

# Doctrinal Beliefs
# Of Jehovah's witnesses

It might be good before we go any further to also look at some of the doctrinal beliefs of the Witnesses, so we can better understand where they are coming from. We will also do a comparison of Christianity's beliefs and that of Jehovah's witnesses.

When an organization claims to be the only true religion and the sole source of correct Bible teaching, we must carefully examine its beliefs. If its doctrines are true, they will be found in the Bible, and its teachings will be consistent and unchanging year after year.

Jehovah's witnesses, however, deny or twist many of the Bible's basic teachings, and their beliefs conflict with those held by orthodox Christians down through the centuries. Let's consider the following comparisons.

*God's Nature.* The Bible teaches that there is only one true God (Isa. 43:10-11; 44:6,8). Father, Son and Holy Spirit are identified as distinct Persons within the Godhead that shares the same essence of deity (Matt. 3:16-17; 2 Cor. 13:14). Throughout the New Testament the Son and the Holy Spirit, as well as the Father are separately identified as God. The attributes and prerogatives of Deity are ascribed to each. (*Son:* Mark 2:5-12; John 20:28; Heb. 1:8; *Holy Spirit:* Acts 5:3-4; 2 Cor. 3:17-18).

*Their View: Jehovah's witnesses deny the tri-unity nature of God and teach that Satan inspires such a belief. They teach that Jehovah, the name of the one true God, corresponds only to God the Father. They also say that Jesus is an angel, Michael. They deny the Holy Spirit is a person, and instead teach He is merely God's active force, analogous to electricity.*

*Jesus Christ.* The Bible teaches that Jesus Christ is God come in the flesh, and is the Creator of *all* things (John 1:1-3, 14; Col. 1:16). While sharing the same essence of God the Father, at the appointed time He laid aside the glory He shared with the Father and took on a human nature (John 17:3-5; Phil. 2:6-11; Col. 2:9). Following His death, Jesus Christ rose bodily from the grave, appeared to and was recognized in His body by over 500 people. This fact was crucial to both the preaching and faith of the early church (Luke 24:39; John 2:19-21; 1 Cor. 15:6, 14).

*Their View: Jehovah's witnesses deny the deity of Jesus Christ and teach that Jesus is a created being. He first existed as Michael the archangel then later was born as a perfect man. Jehovah's Witnesses believe that after Jesus was buried, God disposed of His physical body. Jesus was raised a spirit creature and "material- ized" a fleshly body to make Himself visible. Now in heaven he is again known as Michael the archangel.*

*Salvation.* The Bible teaches that the atoning work of Christ alone provides the solution for man's big problem, which is SIN.

Jesus Christ took the personal sins of all men, past, present and future, in His own body on the tree (1 Pet. 2:24), and as perfect Deity and perfect man He fully met the demands of Divine justice for us (Rom. 3:22-26). Therefore, any and all who receive Him by simple faith (John 1:12; Acts 16:31), can be forgiven, declared righteous and restored to fellowship with God (2 Cor. 5:21; Heb. 7:24-26).

***Their View:*** *Jehovah's witnesses teach that only an elite group of Witnesses, known as "the 144,000," or the "anointed ones" are presently credited with Christ's righteousness. Only the 144,000 are born again and expect to reign with Christ in heaven. For the vast majority of remaining Jehovah's Witnesses, known as the "other sheep" or the "Great Crowd," the atoning sacrifice of Christ only provides "a chance" at eternal life on earth.*

**The Bible**: The Bible teaches that we are saved by grace alone apart from any self-righteous works; salvation is God's gift. There is nothing we can do to contribute to our salvation because apart from Jesus Christ we are "dead in our sins" (Eph. 2:1-9).

***Their View:*** *Jehovah's witnesses teach that we must earn our own salvation; salvation will "depend on one's works." A person must first "come to Jehovah's organization for salvation" and then comply with everything they teach. In this way, a relationship with the Jehovah's Witnesses organization, rather than a personal relationship with Jesus Christ, is presented as the basis of salvation.*

***The Human Spirit & Eternal Punishment.*** The Bible teaches that the human spirit continues to exist consciously after death (Luke 16:19-31; 2 Corinthians 5:6, 8; Philippians 1:23-24; Rev. 6:9-11). Those who have rejected God's gift of eternal life will suffer conscious eternal punishment in the Lake of Fire at the end of the millenium. (Matt. 25:41,46; Rev. 14:10,11; 20:10,15).

*Their View: Jehovah's witnesses deny eternal punishment and teach that man does not have a spirit that survives the death of the body. Witnesses believe that death ends all conscious existence. Hell refers to the grave, and those whom God ultimately judges will be annihilated and simply cease to exist.*

**The Bible.** The Bible teaches that the Holy Spirit's anointing enables individual Christians to understand God's Word and properly apply it to their lives (John 16:13; 1 John 2:27).

*Their View: Jehovah's witnesses teach that the Bible can only be interpreted by the Watchtower Organization, and no individual can learn the truth apart from them.*

Because of books like this and other exposure of the Witnesses false predictions many faithful witnesses have expressed concerns about the organization. Because of that, the Watchtower Society has responded by publishing articles and books in which they admit they have made mistakes in their historical predictions and doctrinal teaching.

They excuse these errors by attributing them to human fallibility and by saying the Watchtower Society has never claimed to be inspired by God. This is a bold deception, since past Watchtower magazines are referred to as "God's message," and have carried instructions from Jehovah in quotation marks.

A Watchtower magazine as recently as August 1, 1995 stated, "Jehovah particularly teaches his people by means of a weekly study of the Bible, using *The Watchtower* as a teaching aid."

Right in the middle of World War II, in 1943, Watchtower Society, Vice President Frederick Franz, and President Nathan H. Knorr provided the following testimony under oath in a court of law that the content of *The Watchtower* comes directly from God.

I have included here the Cross-examination of Frederick W. Franz in the case of *Olin Moyle v. WTB&TS,* 1943, Sections #2596-2597, p. 866.

I personally knew Olin Moyle. For 22 years I lived within one mile of his home. I walked by his home every day on my way to school. He lived in the town I grew up in, Johnson Creek, Wisconsin. He was an attorney, and a very humble man. For years the Watchtower Society tried to ruin his reputation.

Olin Moyle was an honorable man. In one instance he approached Judge Rutherford about the concern of so much alcohol flowing among the young workers and staff at the Headquarters in Brooklyn, N.Y.

Rutherford, himself an alcoholic, chastised Moyle, and after Moyle was no longer a part of the Watchtower Bible and Tract Society. Rutherford and the Society tried to smear Moyle's character, and tried to paint Moyle as the person with a drinking problem.

From what I observed of Olin Moyle, he never drank at all! Moyle was so slandered by the Society, that he sued them and won!! He was a very pleasant person. He always had a smile for you. I just wish I could talk to him today!! Olin Moyle has passed away.

So lets observe the transcript of an actual court case in which Brother Knorr admitted that Jehovah was the editor of the Watchtower and that the Watchtower could be equated with the Bible, the Word of God. Doesn't that sound strange!! I thought so. Read on!!

**Q.** At any rate, Jehovah God is now the editor of the paper [*The Watchtower*], is that right?

**A.** He is today the editor of the paper.

**Q.** How long has He been editor of the paper?

**A.** Since its inception he has been guiding it. This can be found in the Cross-examination of Nathan Homer Knorr in the case of *Olin Moyle v. WTB&TS*, 1943, Section #4421, p. 1474. The questioning goes on.

**Q.** In fact, it [*The Watchtower*] is set forth directly as God's Word, isn't it?

**A.** Yes, as His word.

**Q.** Without any qualification whatsoever?

**A.** That is right.

Many people remain unaware of these damaging facts, and the Witnesses continue to grow in number, distributing massive amounts of deceptive literature. In spite of its past failures and recent claims to not be inspired, the Watchtower Society still demands complete loyalty and continues to predict Armageddon is coming soon with sure annihilation for anyone who does not join the organization or for anyone who leaves its ranks.

Even with a history marred by manipulation and false prophecies, the Watchtower Society still claims to be the only one teaching the truth.

**Evidently Jehovah changes His mind!!**

The Watchtower Bible and Tract Society claims to be Jehovah's organization and God's only channel of spiritual instruction for today. It says the Bible is an "organizational book" and cannot be understood by individuals no matter how sincere they are.

But how can we trust our eternal destiny to an organization that during its brief time in existence has accumulated such a woeful history of doctrinal contradictions and flip-flops? Consider the following examples of ever-changing Watchtower theology.

In 1975 the Watchtower Bible and Tract Society taught that the man who sows the seed in the parable of the mustard seed (Matthew 13) is Satan. Later that same year the Watchtower Bible and Tract Society taught that this sower was Jesus.

A similar incident occurred in 1978, when the Watchtower Bible and Tract Society identified the "Alpha and Omega" of Revelation 22:12-13 as Jehovah (that is, God the Father), and then five weeks later taught these verses referred to Jesus.

The Watchtower Society's failure to correctly interpret the Bible is most clearly seen in their doctrinal flip-flops. First they teach position **A**, then they change to position **B**, claiming God has given them "new light." Later on, however, they revert back to their old teaching (position **A**) and in some cases change once again to position **B**. Here are some examples.

*The 'Lord' in Romans 10:12-16*
1903 - 'Lord' refers to Jesus.
1940 - 'Lord' refers to Jehovah.
1978 - 'Lord' refers to Jesus.

1980 - 'Lord' refers to Jehovah.

### Resurrection of the Men of Sodom
1879 - They will be resurrected.
1952 - They will not be resurrected.
1965 - They will be resurrected.
1988 - They will not be resurrected.

### Separating 'sheep and goats' (Matt. 25:31-46)
1919 - will take place after the time of tribulation.
1923 - is taking place now, before the tribulation.
1995 - will take place after the tribulation.

### 'Higher Powers' of Romans 13:1
1916 - 'Higher powers' refers to governments.
1943 - 'Higher powers' refers to Jehovah God & Jesus Christ.
1964 - 'Higher powers' refers to governments.

So the question I had to answer and you will too is: How can we base our decisions that affect our eternal life, on an organization that demands loyalty in our belief in them, yet cannot make up its mind as to what Jehovah is telling us.

Jehovah's witnesses when they change their ideas, say they are getting "New Light" from Jehovah. But let's be honest. What kind of light are they getting when they take a position, rescind the decision and then embrace it again, only to rescind it again, only to embrace it again!! You call that "New Light"? I call it crazy. You might want to call it deception or confusion!!

Lord, give us the wisdom to see the real truth of the Bible!

# CHAPTER 4

# Journey Of A Man Who Loves God

## (Or otherwise known as the Long Chapter!)

B efore we get into the "meat" of this book, "The 20 Questions Jehovah's witnesses Cannot Answer", let me give you a brief sketch of my life to show you where I am really coming from.

As mentioned in the introduction, I was a Jehovah's witness for 30 years.

My mother was converted to Jehovah's witnesses when I was 5 years old. I always had some kind of a love of God, and while my dad initially would not accept the Witness religion, I followed my mom to the Kingdom Hall every week. I also went out in service when I was very young. I thought that my mom had found the "truth".

I lived in Wisconsin, and it was in that state that I grew up in the organization. I was a "good" Jehovah's witness. That means I served as an Elder, Presiding Overseer, Theocratic Ministry School Overseer and all of the other rotating positions held by elders at the time I was a Witness.

I pioneered from time to time, and I was a good "publisher". That means I put in at least 10 hours per month in field service, which means going door to door with the Watchtower publications.

I realize that the terms of the Watchtower Society are continually changing, but I write this book, using the language of the Witnesses when I was there.

I spoke at most circuit assemblies, many of the district assemblies and even some of the major conventions. In fact, in my office I have a large picture of me speaking at a circuit assembly when I was just 9 years old. It's quite a picture. I was so cute!!

I loved the Witness organization. I was good friends with many elders and ministerial servants among many Jehovah's witnesses congregations. They are good people. I believe they love God and want to do what is right. I cherish the memories of their friendship.

I was great friends with many Circuit and District Overseers. I still have fond memories of them and pray that they will come to know Jesus Christ as their Lord and Savior. I was especially fond of a District Overseer named Ruben. I pray for him often that he will come to know the real Jesus. The people I remember are wonderful people. They were very dedicated and I thank them for their friendship.

I had a very close friend name Ken. He was like a brother. We shared life's experiences together. I was there for him during his times of trouble with his first marriage. He is another one I pray will come to know Jesus some day.

As mentioned earlier in this book, I personally met Brother Knorr, the third president of the Watchtower Society. In fact I had him in my home when I lived in Milwaukee. I loved the man.

I still have deep feelings for Jehovah's witnesses and many of the people that I know. Because we chose to leave the Witnesses over doctrinal issues, they no longer talk to my wife, or me but we still have a great love for them.

After my wife and I left the Witnesses, amazingly only a handful of people called me to see why we had left the Witnesses. I guess their friendship was not as deep as we had anticipated! Maybe for them it is good they didn't call me. Because everyone who called me, to see what was going on, eventually became a Christian!! I praise God for that.

Now that we have had some time to think about Jehovah's witnesses, we have discovered that many are dysfunctional when it comes to personal relationships.

While the Witnesses put on the pretense of loving one another, let someone fall from their graces, and you will find they are eager to stop association with people who once were their *deepest friends*!!

But I want you to fully understand something. I loved Jehovah's witnesses.

In the mid 1970's my wife and I decided that Wisconsin was too cold. I had been born and raised there and even though I was still a Green Bay Packer fan, I couldn't take the cold anymore. So, we decided to move to Phoenix.

It was while we were in Phoenix, that I had been selected to give an important message at a Jehovah's witness district convention being held in that city. The Watchtower Society had sent me an outline, and I was to deliver that message at the convention.

The theme of the message was "Son's of God". In the vernacular of Jehovah's witnesses, Sons of God, only applies to the 144,000 class.

As you may or may not know, Jehovah's witnesses believe there are 2 classes of people in their organization. There is the 144,000 class which they believe go to heaven after they die. Then there is the Great Crowd, which is the majority of Jehovah's witnesses, who believe that when they die they will live forever on earth. Only the 144,000 have instant life after death in heaven.

The Great Crowd, who the Jehovah's witnesses began picking in 1935 go out of existence when they die. And their hope is that Jehovah will resurrect them during the millennium, or thousand year reign of Jesus.

The problem with all of this is you can't prove it according to the Bible. The Witnesses believe that when they die, their spirit, their breath goes out of the body and they pass out of existence. Listen to what the Bible says about the spirit.

In the Biblical, Christian Doctrine, the Spirit lives after you die and you, your living self, your spirit, goes to heaven to be with the Lord.

That is why Stephen, the first Christian Martyr looked into heaven in the Books of Acts and said: "Lord Jesus, receive my spirit".

Then according to the Bible, when Christ returns, He indeed makes us a glorified body, in which our living spirit will dwell. It will truly be us. It will be our living spirit and personality, living in a new glorified body that will resemble the glorified body that our Lord Jesus has. Praise God. Now that is hope!!

But we are getting ahead of the story. So let me go back to my journey out of the Witnesses.

I was given this talk to give at a Jehovah's witness convention in Phoenix. I was to talk about the Son's of God. When I started doing research on the subject, it took me into the book of Romans. And it was in the book of Romans that I made some startling discoveries.

For example, in Romans 8:14, it says in the Witness Bible, The New World Translation, that all who are led by God's spirit are Sons of God. In other words, in the Witness jargon, all who are led by God's spirit are members of the 144,000 class, who according to them are the only Sons of God.

That scripture in Romans created a big problem for my fellow Jehovah's witnesses and me. I had always prayed for Jehovah's spirit to lead me. But, according to that scripture in Romans 8, if Jehovah did lead me, then who was I? It says: I would have to be a "Son of God".

As a Jehovah's witness, I was a member of the Great Crowd. I was not interested in going to heaven. I wanted to live on earth forever. Yet the scripture had to be true. "All who are led by the spirit of God are Sons of God." All means All!!

So I thought to myself. Hmm. That's strange. I wonder if there is something else here that doesn't add up. So I began to read the entire Bible book of Romans. I found some interesting things.

In Romans 3 I found that I was a sinner. Romans 3:23 says: "For all have sinned and come short of the glory of God." Romans 5:12 says "Therefore, just as sin entered the world through one man, and death through sin, in this way death spread to all men, because all sinned."

I noticed in Romans 6:23 an interesting verbiage. It said: "The wages of sin is death, but **the gift of God is eternal life through Christ Jesus our Lord.**"

What I found here was the key to my salvation. It was pretty important!!

Up to this point, I thought that I was saved by being a good

Jehovah's witnesses. If I wanted to live forever in the New world: I needed to trust Jehovah's organization, go to the meetings, go out in service, live a good life, and hope I made it into the new world.

That was my gospel message as a Jehovah's witness. That is how I, a member of the Great Crowd, was going to get eternal life. Basically if I worked hard at it and didn't mess up, Jehovah would reward me with life on this earth.

That is still the way a Jehovah's witness gains life. Ask the next Jehovah's witness that knocks on your door to give you the equation for living forever. You will find interesting answers.

Now as I read those scriptures in Romans, it began to be clear to me that eternal life is a GIFT from God, and it is only available by putting faith in His Son, Jesus Christ. The Bible doesn't say that I have to work real hard, be good, go to Jehovah's witnesses meetings and put trust in the organization of Jehovah's witnesses .

The Bible says eternal life is a gift through Jesus Christ. What is important to understand here is that a gift is free. You don't work for a gift. When you work, you receive a wage. Jehovah's witnesses must "work" for their salvation. Under those circumstances then, their salvation isn't a gift, it is a wage. This is contradictory to what the Bible says!

Is your salvation based on being a gift or is it based on being a wage. If your salvation is due to a wage, or something you have done to earn it, then you don't have salvation. You have a religion that will get you eternal separation from God!!

I found some other interesting things in Romans that I had never been aware of. There was a term in the New World Translation (the Jehovah's witnesses Bible) that I was not aware of. The term was "Declared Righteous." I looked up the verses that contained that phrase in the New World Translation, in other Bibles, and I found the word they used for declared righteous was justification.

As a Witness I had never heard or studied that term. I wondered what it meant. I read the scriptures that contained the word with extreme interest. In fact, if you the reader of this book, can grasp what I am about to explain, it will change your life!

Lets look at a few of the scriptures containing the words "declared righteous" and see what these mean, and why it is so important for us to understand that term..

The first scripture I noticed was that salvation scripture!! Rom 3:23 "For all have sinned and fall short of the glory of God." That is an important explanation of mankind's plight.

But look at verse 24. Rom 3:24 "They are **declared righteous** freely by His grace through the redemption that is in Christ Jesus."

Wow, I didn't understand what declared righteous meant, but it sure sounded pretty awesome to me!! "Declared righteous by His grace through the redemption that is in Christ Jesus!!" That sounded like something wonderful happened to me when I put faith in the redemptive value of the sacrifice of Jesus Christ. Hmmm, what is going on here?

What was to follow would change me forever!! I got to Romans chapter 5 verse 1. It says: "Therefore having been declared righteous by faith, we have peace with God through our Lord Jesus Christ." Wow! Peace with God through faith in Jesus Christ! And the scripture says, it happens after being declared righteous! I thought, I must be on to something!!

Then I found Romans 5, starting at verse 8!

Rom 5:8 But God proves His own love for us in that while we were still sinners Christ died for us!

Rom 5:9 Much more then, since we have now been declared righteous by His blood, we will be saved through Him from wrath.

Rom 5:10 For if, while we were enemies, we were reconciled to God through the death of His Son, *then how* much more, having been reconciled, will we be saved by His life!

I was about ready to jump out of my skin!! This scripture defined me!! I was a sinner. And while I was a sinner Christ died for me!! Then I was declared righteous by His blood and saved through Him from wrath!! I wasn't going to make it through Armageddon by myself. I wasn't going to earn salvation by working hard, I was saved by the blood of Christ and by putting faith in Jesus!!

By faith, I could be reconciled to God, declared righteous and saved from wrath. I could have peace with God and I would become one of His children and live forever with Him in heaven!! This gift and promise was open to everyone, not just the 144,000!!

Hallelujah!! Being declared righteous means that because of my faith in Jesus Christ, when God looks at me, He no longer looks at Chuck the sinner. When God looks at me, He looks at Chuck the sinner and sees, Jesus the righteous!!

When I accept Christ, God imputes or gives to me the righteousness of Christ. I can't live by my own righteousness, because I don't have any. I am a sinner. That's why my works mean nothing. In fact, Paul said that all of his works were like rubbish! So Christ had to die to relieve me of my sin and cover me with His righteousness, so that a Holy God could once again deal with me as a son.

In Jehovah's witnesses teaching, being declared righteous only applies to the 144,000. That is why according to the Watchtower Bible and Tract Society, the Great Crowd are dead in God's eyes, which will be explained later!

The truth of the matter is that ANYONE and EVERYONE who puts faith in Jesus Christ is saved, declared righteous and is a son of God, with heaven as their destiny!!

You can't say you accept Christ and think you are going to live on the earth. Salvation doesn't work that way!! All who are saved, all who accept Christ go to heaven to live with Christ forever. I challenge you to find anything in the New Testament that contradicts that!!

Now, I wanted to make sure that my salvation was based on faith and not on an organization, so I thought it was important to read the rest of the New Testament to see if it substantiated my findings in Romans.

Was my salvation by faith in Jesus, or was it by following an organization. It had to be one or the other. So I started to read the New Testament.

In Matthew and Luke, I found in the birth of Jesus story, the fact that He is the Savior! He wasn't just some Archangel that came to earth to die for the 144,000. He was the Son of God, Emmanuel, God, with us, who came to this earth to be the Savior of those who would believe!!

In John, I found that Jesus says that HE is the way! Jesus was the only way to life. I found nothing in the Bible that ever says that an organization is the way of life. I challenge every reader of this book to prove me wrong. The word organization cannot be found in the Bible!! Salvation is not found in an organization. According to Holy Scripture, salvation is always only found in putting faith in Jesus. It's all about Jesus!

In Acts 16:31 I found this beautiful scripture. It contained the whole of the gospel and the key to eternal life. It says that ALL who believe on Jesus are saved. All who believe!! No mention of an organization. It is all about belief in Jesus.

In Ephesians chapter 2 I found some really hard hitting words. As a Witness, I was sure that I was saved by good works and by working hard. But Ephesians 2:8,9 says: "We are saved by grace through faith, and not of ourselves, lest we should boast".

Think about it. How haughty I was as a Jehovah's witness. How could I ever think that my meager good works would ever be good enough to cover my sins and earn me salvation. What was I thinking!! How could I be so clueless!! Who did I think I was to be able to, on my own, earn salvation and any merit with Jehovah!!

The Bible says here in Ephesians, without reservation, that we are not saved by our good works. If we were, then we could forever boast about how good we are. We are simply saved by putting faith in Jesus Christ.

And then in First Corinthians I found what the REAL GOSPEL IS. In First Corinthians chapter 15 verses 1-4, Paul identifies the gospel as: Jesus coming to this earth, living a sinless life, dying on the cross, being in the grave 3 days, and then being resurrected on the third day. All who believe in Him are saved.

How contrary to what I was talking about when I went door to door, spreading the Jehovah's witnesses Gospel. I never talked about Jesus. It was all about the name Jehovah. And that doctrine has not changed. I have Witnesses stop at my door regularly and they never mention Jesus. It's all about Jehovah.

Why don't they mention Jesus? Because Jehovah's witnesses have not personally accepted Him as their Lord and Savior. They are not declared righteous. They are dead in God's eyes and are not counted worthy to live with Jesus in Heaven, because they don't know Him. That is not my thought about them, that is the thought of the Watchtower Bible and Tract Society about them!! That is what the Jehovah's witnesses teach about the Great Crowd!! The Great Crowd has nothing without Jesus. That is why they are second-class citizens!!

In Philippians Paul says there is no other name in which people get saved, than the name of Jesus! It's not the name Jehovah, that saves. Nowhere in the New Testament, can you find one scripture that says, by putting faith in the name of Jehovah that you will be saved and will live forever on earth!! I found in Philippians that Paul said there is only one name that saves people and that name is Jesus!! There is no other way to salvation.

When a person accepts Jesus as Lord and Savior, guess what happens. He or She becomes declared righteous and becomes a Son of God, because, ALL who are led by the Spirit of God are sons of God.

Wow!! It came around full circle!! It all came back to Romans Chapter 8!!

Now if the date 1935 is not in the Bible, and if nothing is ever mentioned in the Bible about following an organization, and if working hard for my salvation was not mentioned in the Bible, then as a Jehovah's witness, where did I get these ideas. Or more important, where did the Jehovah's witnesses get their ideas? Research will tell us that most of those ideas came from Judge Rutherford, the second president of the Watchtower Society.

Charles Russell, the founder of Jehovah's witnesses actually believed that both the 144,000 and the Great Crowd went to heaven when they died. In his writings, Charles Russell condemned organizations that claimed to be the only ones with the truth about God. Ironically it was through Russell that the Witness organization began to be formed.

Judge Rutherford built on that foundation and then went with the idea that Jehovah was using an organization to dispense the truth to true followers, and naturally it was the organization of Jehovah's witnesses. It was Judge Rutherford, who came up with the idea that God had stopped picking those who would go to heaven in 1935.

According to Rutherford, from then on, God was only going to pick the Great Crowd, people who would live on the earth. Like most of his decisions, they were only his decisions, not founded in the Bible.

Is Judge Rutherford a man whose decisions you really would want to trust and follow?

According to people that knew him, Judge Rutherford, the second president of the Watchtower Society, was an alcoholic and died of liver disease in San Diego at the Watchtower home called Beth Sarim. I think many of Rutherford's theological decisions must have been made in a drunken stupor!! As you can tell, he is not my favorite person! I really believe that it is because of his error and his demonic way of living that so many witnesses are deceived today.

Anyhow, I was stuck in a quandary. I loved Jehovah's witnesses, but their beliefs could not be substantiated by the Bible. So I decided to investigate each one of Jehovah's witnesses beliefs. I would use the Bible as my only guide.

If I could prove a doctrine of Jehovah's witnesses by the Bible, I would continue to believe it. If I could not prove a doctrine of Jehovah's witnesses by the Bible, then I would discard that doctrine from my belief system.

I knew I was entering forbidden waters. I was entering into an area that could lead me away from the organization of Jehovah's witnesses. However I had to live the truth. I could not let an organization or anyone else keep my family and me from living by the real truth. So I began to investigate further. The way I would proceed would be profound but quite easy.

I would take each doctrine of Jehovah's witnesses and try to prove it right by the Bible. I was not going to try to prove the doctrine wrong. I wanted to prove it right. Because you must remember, I loved the organization of Jehovah's witnesses. I wanted to remain in the organization.

And really, I thought I knew that I could prove the doctrines of Jehovah's witnesses right. After all, I had given that organization 30 years of my life. I couldn't have been wrong all those years. I was about to be surprised!!

One of the things that the Lord impressed upon me to do, was to have a helper analyze the doctrines with me. So who else better to engage in this than my wife, Deanna? I developed a system. I would find scriptures that would be problem areas for backing up my beliefs about the Witnesses. I would let Deanna read the same scriptures. I would not tell her what the scriptures were saying to me, I wanted to hear first what the scriptures meant to her. If they meant the same to her as they did to me, then we would have a match!! That would be a pretty good confirmation that we were on the right track.

If I didn't get the same answer from Deanna that I was getting from the scripture, I would go back and do more study. It was amazing how almost all the time, scripture was saying the same thing to Deanna as it was to me. So I began my journey for truth.

My journey took several years, but briefly here is what I found. This is not a complete list, but it is a list of troubling doctrines of the Witnesses that could not be proved by the Bible.

First, I wanted to prove that the Great Crowd would live on the earth forever. I thought this would be an easy one to prove. But I found no scripture that said that. The fact of the matter is, I found a powerful scripture in **Revelation 19:1. It says the Great Crowd are in Heaven!!** It completely destroys Witness doctrine!! I couldn't believe it. Black and white. The Great Crowd are in Heaven. Grab a New World Translation and read it for yourselves.

I wanted to prove that only 144,000 go to heaven. Again the Bible provided no proof. The scriptures dealing with 144,000 in Revelation chapters 7 and 14, are dealing specifically with Jews. The 144,000 have nothing to do with Jehovah's witnesses organization!

I believed that Jehovah's name was the most important name. I was amazed that there is not one scripture in the New Testament that says that. Rather, the most important name in the New Testament was, you guessed it, Jesus. I talk about that later.

Wouldn't you think that if Jehovah's name was that important, that at least one time, Jesus or any of the disciples would have told us to go door to door and tell everyone that Jehovah's name is the most important name.

It just makes sense. And yet for years, I blindly followed the organization of Jehovah's witnesses, spreading the word that Jehovah was the most important name in the universe.

But as we saw earlier in this chapter, Philippians tells us that Jesus is the most important name. There can't be 2 most important names!!

The most important area that I really ran into a problem when I was trying to prove the Witnesses right, was in the area of salvation. I have discussed this earlier, and you will continue to see this theme throughout this book. As I have already explained, Jehovah's witnesses are a works righteousness religion.

The gospel message is very simple. We are all sinners, because we inherited sin from our first parents Adam and Eve. There is no way on our own that we can get rid of that sin. We cannot conquer sin, by doing good works. The New Testament tells us that there is only one way for salvation and that is Jesus Christ. It starts with John 3:16. "God loved us so much that He sent His son and all who believe on Him will be saved!"

Salvation has nothing to do with our works. Salvation has already been accomplished through the death and resurrection of Jesus. All we need to do is to believe in Him and we receive forgiveness of our sins and the free gift of salvation. When I understood this, I could no longer remain a member of Jehovah's witnesses. It now became a life or death matter. If I remained under the belief system of Jehovah's witnesses, I would lose eternal life. And not only me but my family. So it was a painful, yet necessary decision.

Jehovah's witnesses organization is a death dealing organization. Christianity is a life saving belief. Let me emphasize that fact in a powerful way.

In my study, I came across the scripture in Revelation Chapter 20 verse 5. The Bible is talking about what happens at the end of the millennium. It is there that the scripture says in the New World

Translation: "And the rest of the dead came to life at the end of the thousand years."

I have briefly mentioned this point previously, but here is the Jehovah's witnesses interpretation of the people in this scripture, called, "the rest of the dead." After understanding this, why would anyone find belonging to the Witnesses attractive!!

According to the belief of Jehovah's witnesses, "the rest of the dead" really is the Great Crowd. That is how the Witnesses themselves interpret this scripture! Their older book, Aid to Bible Understanding explicitly explains this point under the topic of Great Crowd.

As I explained previously, the Bible says that when you accept Christ, you are alive in Christ and will live forever with Him. The Bible says that when you accept Christ, you are declared righteous or justified.

What that means is, when you accept Christ as your Lord and Savior, God imputes or gives you the righteousness of Christ. When you sin, God no longer looks at you the sinner, but sees the righteousness of Christ and forgives your sin. When you accept Christ, your spirit comes alive and you no longer need to fear death, because when you die, your spirit goes to live with God.

The Witnesses believe this also. The problem is, they apply it only to the 144,000. In the Witness belief system, only the 144,000 are declared righteous. Only the 144,000 are alive in God's eyes. Only the 144,000 go immediately to heaven after they die.

Now get this. The Great Crowd in the eyes of Jehovah's witnesses are dead in God's eyes. I will talk a lot about this so get used to it. It is a very important subject! Because the Watchtower Society says the Great Crowd are not declared righteous, that means that when God looks at the Great Crowd, they are still sinners. More importantly to the Great Crowd, they must understand that according to Witness doctrine, when God looks at them they are dead. Remember. This is the Watchtower's Belief system!!

You need to understand that the organization of Jehovah's witnesses takes life away from all those who are members of the Great Crowd. That is 99% of their members!

Now let me ask you. Do you really want to be a part of an organization that keeps you dead in God's eyes? What kind of a religion is that!! I thought religion was formed to give its adherents life!! Jehovah's witnesses organization is a dealer in death to its members. How terrible!!

When I understood this I was mad, hurt and upset. The organization that I loved made me dead in Gods eyes. But that wasn't the worst of it.

They not only had me dead in God's eyes, but they also had my wife and children dead! I could no longer tolerate their death dealing beliefs.

The organization of Jehovah's witnesses was condemning me and my family to death. How ridiculous. Don't let an organization keep you and your family dead in God's eyes. Break free and worship the King of Kings and Lord of Lord's, Jesus Christ.

Now, I also found many other things that Jehovah's witnesses taught and believed that just couldn't be backed up by the Bible. It is those things taught by Jehovah's witnesses as the gospel truth and that can't be backed up by scripture that is the basis for the 20 questions that Jehovah's witnesses cannot answer.

So lets get busy and reveal the 20 questions.

May God Bless your journey.

# CHAPTER 5

# The Plan Of Salvation

I got a call one day from my friend who was a Jehovah's witness in Milwaukee. He was so upset I left the Witnesses. I told him the plan of salvation and that I had found Jesus. He mocked my new found beliefs and then he hung up.

About 2 years later, I got another call from my friend in Milwaukee. He said: "Chuck I have called to apologize for being so nasty to you on the phone." And then he said those words that made my heart jump. He said: "I have accepted Jesus Christ. I am now your brother in Christ." Praise God!! I am so proud of him!!

As you can tell by what I have already mentioned in this book, the issue of salvation is a very important issue. So as we start with the 20 questions, we will naturally start with that subject. As we address this first question we are looking for just one answer please. We are not even looking for many scriptures to prove the Great Crowd's point.

We are really looking for just ONE scripture for them to base their religion on.

**So, the First Question is: WHERE IS THE PLAN OF SALVA-TION IN THE BIBLE FOR THE GREAT CROWD.**

According to the Watchtower Society, the plan of salvation for the Great Crowd is to go to meetings, go out in service, be good, work hard and then HOPE you will not be destroyed by God at the battle of Armageddon. Where do you find that in the Bible? There is only one way of salvation mentioned in the Bible.

First, Jesus says that He is the only way. There is not one way for the 144,000 and another way for the Great Crowd. The fact that Jesus is the only way to salvation is found throughout the New Testament.

Acts 16:31 says: Believe on the Lord Jesus and you will be saved.

John 3:16, says: Believe on the Lord Jesus and be saved.

Romans 6:24 says that we receive life by the free gift, Jesus Christ.

The real gospel is that we are all sinners and need to be forgiven of our sin. This is contrary to what Jehovah's witnesses teach as their doctrine. They feel that there is this God named Jehovah that is so consumed with Himself that all He wants "His people" to do is go door to door to tell people that God's name is Jehovah. The problem with that doctrine is it is not found in the New Testament.

The gospel as found in the New Testament is explained by Paul in 1 Corinthians 15: 1-4.

1Co 15:1 And, brothers, I declare to you the gospel which I

preached to you, which also you have received, and in which you stand;

1Co 15:2 by which you also are being kept safe, if you hold fast the word which I preached to you, unless you believed in vain.

1Co 15:3 For I delivered to you first of all that which I also received, that Christ died for our sins, according to the Scriptures,

1Co 15:4 and that He was buried, and that He rose again the third day according to the Scriptures;

That is the gospel that makes a difference. It is so important that we proclaim the gospel of 1 Corinthians 15 that Paul said this in Galatians, Chapter 1.

Gal 1:6 I marvel that you so soon are being moved away from Him who called you into *the* grace of Christ, to another gospel,

Gal 1:7 which is not another, but some are troubling you, and desiring to pervert the gospel of Christ.

Gal 1:8 **But even if we or an angel from Heaven preach a gospel to you beside what we preached to you, let him be accursed.**

Gal 1:9 As we said before, and now I say again, **If anyone preaches a gospel to you beside what you have received, let him be accursed.**

So there we have it. One Gospel and only one Biblical salvation. "Believe on the Lord Jesus and you will be saved." That's it. For the Great Crowd, 144,000, and everyone else on the planet, there is one way for salvation and that is believe on the Lord Jesus and you will be saved.

Now, what is interesting, is when you accept Christ, the Bible says that you become a child of God, an heir with Christ, Alive, Priest and King. According to Jehovah's witnesses, none of that applies to the Great Crowd. In Witness theology that only applies to the 144,000. So again we ask you, where then is the plan of salvation for the members of the Great Crowd?

If there is no plan of salvation that specifically says in the Bible that: "This is the plan of salvation for the Great Crowd", then you really have 2 choices.

Choice Number 1: There is no plan of salvation for the Great Crowd, so you are doomed.

Choice Number 2: The plan of salvation for the Great Crowd is the same as the plan of salvation for the 144,000. If that is the case then your destination must also be the same!

The truth is, there is only one plan of salvation and that is believing on Jesus. When you do that, you will live forever with your Lord and Savior in heaven or wherever He goes! Now that's really the gospel. The only one!

It is interesting that at the time of the writing of this book, there is another book that has been published by the Watchtower Society that is their book of the hour.

The book is called "Draw Close to Jehovah." In the book there are 31 chapters. The idea of the book is we are to draw close to the Father, who in the Witness language is Jehovah.

The book tells the reader to draw close to Jehovah, but doesn't explain that the only way we can even get to the Father is through Jesus Christ.

Listen to what Jesus said about drawing closer to the Father. In John 6:40, Jesus says: "For this is the will of My Father: that everyone who sees the Son and believes in Him may have eternal life, and I will raise him up on the last day." Instead of showing everyone that the way to the Father is through Jesus Christ, the book concludes with how we are to gain life and draw close to the Father.

The last chapter of the book "Draw close to Jehovah" reads:

> "May you respond to Jehovah's love now, by loving him with your whole heart, soul, mind and strength." (Mark 12:29,30) May your love be loyal and steadfast. May the decisions that you make every day, from the smallest to the greatest, all reflect the same guiding principle-that you will always choose the path that leads you to a stronger relationship with your heavenly Father. Above all, may you draw ever closer to Jehovah and may he draw ever closer throughout all eternity."

Did you notice, it all depends on you. Your access to Jehovah depends on how well you behave, choose and decide. In the Witness way of thinking that means being loyal to Jehovah's organization. But look what Jesus said in John 14:6: "I am the way, the truth, and the life. No one comes to the Father except through Me."

In the Witness book, Draw Close to Jehovah, the Witness book says we need to do it on our own!! In my personal, humble opinion, I think the Witness book should have closed with words something like this:

May you respond to the Father's love by accepting His Son Jesus? By accepting Christ, you will become a Son of God and be lead by the Holy Spirit to draw closer to the Father.

Because you know Jesus, the Father will lead you to a closer relationship with Him, and no matter if you die today, or in 100 years, through Christ, you will draw closer to your Heavenly Father through eternity, as one of His children.

Now that is hope and encouragement!!

I wonder if the Watchtower Bible and Tract Society would let me start writing their books for them!! Judge Rutherford would turn over in his grave!!

# CHAPTER 6

# A Closer Look At The Great Crowd

Questions 2,3 and 4 all continue to deal with the Great Crowd. The story goes that in 1935, Judge Rutherford, the second president of the Watchtower society had a problem. Only 144,000 were supposed to go to heaven, but there were more than 144,000 Jehovah's witnesses. So that is why he came up with the idea that the Great Crowd was another group and that they would live on the earth.

So as we discuss these next questions about the Great Crowd, we are looking for some pretty simple answers to the questions.

**Question two is: Where Specifically does the Bible say: "The Great Crowd will live on the earth."**

It is truly amazing that this most important doctrine for Jehovah's witnesses cannot be found in the Bible. The Witnesses use Revelation 7 as their proof text that the Great Crowd will live on the earth, but that scripture actually proves just the opposite.

The first President of the Watchtower Society, Charles Russell believed that the Great Crowd was not an earthly class but rather a heavenly class. He also interpreted Revelation chapter 7, as putting the Great Crowd in heaven. Let's look for a moment at the "Great Crowd" account in Revelation chapter 7.

Rev 7:9 After these things I looked, and lo, a great multitude, which no man could number, out of all nations and kindreds and people and tongues, stood before the throne and before the Lamb, clothed with white robes, with palms in their hands.

Rev 7:10 And they cried with a loud voice, saying, Salvation to our God sitting on the throne, and to the Lamb.

Rev 7:11 And all the angels stood around the throne, and the elders, and the four living creatures, and they fell before the throne on their faces and worshiped God,

Rev 7:12 saying, Amen! Blessing and glory and wisdom and thanksgiving and honor and power and might *be* to our God forever and ever. Amen.

Rev 7:13 And one of the elders answered, saying to me, Who are these who are arrayed in white robes, and from where do they come?

Rev 7:14 And I said to him, Sir, you know. And he said to me, these are the ones who came out of the great tribulation and have washed their robes, and have whitened them in the blood of the Lamb.

Rev 7:15 Therefore they are before the throne of God, and they serve Him day and night in His temple. And He sitting on the throne will dwell among them.

In verse 9 we notice right away that the Great Crowd is in heaven. This is a heavenly scene. The heavenly throne and the Lamb are there. The Great Crowd is standing before the throne.

In verse 11 we see other heavenly creation. There are angels, the elders and the four living creatures. These are always spoken of in Revelation as heavenly creatures. Notice what they did. They fell before the heavenly throne and worshiped God who was there.

But verse 13 presents a powerful question. One of the elders asks, "Who are these who are arrayed in white robes, and from where do they come?" That would be a silly question if this was an earthly scene.

The reason the elder wanted to know where this Great Crowd, is from, is that they were strangers to the territory. They were strangers to heaven. If this was an earthly scene the answer to the question might have been, New York or California!!

But, notice the answer in verse 14. *These are the ones that come out of the great tribulation.* These are earthly tribulation saints, who still go to heaven, but they have to go through the tribulation, because they accepted Christ after the tribulation began.

Notice their salvation. Verse 14 says this crowd have washed their robes and whitened them in the blood of the lamb. They didn't believe an organization for salvation, they accepted Christ for salvation!! Then in verse 15 it says they are before the throne of God, and they serve Him DAY and NIGHT in His temple. These are heavenly people. They don't sleep. Earthly people sleep. But this Great Crowd serves in the temple, DAY and NIGHT, without need for sleep. In verse 15 Revelation says that they serve God day and night in His temple.

The Greek word for temple, and you can look this up in the Witness Greek Interlinear Bible, is the *divine habitation of God*. Where does God habitate? God habitates or lives or resides in what we know as Heaven. It is obvious. The Great Crowd is in heaven.

**Question 3 asks: So do Jehovah's witnesses teach a lie that the Great Crowd will live on the earth?** It certainly appears so!!

But question number 4 sinks the Witnesses belief that the Great Crowd will live on earth.

**Question number Four is: Why does the Watchtower Society say that the Great Crowd will live on the earth, when Revelation 19:1 says that <u>the Great Crowd is in Heaven?</u>**

Notice what Revelation 19:1 says. It identifies for us, where the Great Crowd are to reside.

Rev 19:1 And after these things I heard a great sound of **a great crowd in Heaven**, saying, Hallelujah! Salvation and glory and honor and the power to the Lord our God!

There is no doubt. The Great Crowd of the Bible live in Heaven.

I was a Jehovah's witness for 30 years and never read that scripture in Revelation 19! How can anyone, say that the Great Crowd is an earthly crowd.

What is interesting is that there is no scripture that says the Great Crowd will live on the earth. Here we find a scripture that says just the opposite. "I heard a great sound of a Great Crowd in heaven."

It just doesn't get any more plain than that!! This question alone, by itself, should be enough to send the Witnesses, the members of the Great Crowd, packing from their organization. This is a serious doctrine to have wrong, because it affects 99% of Jehovah's witnesses.

Since 1935, when the alcoholic president of the Watchtower Society, Judge Rutherford, made the decision that the majority of Jehovah's witnesses should live on the earth, Jehovah's witnesses have been living a lie. When will they wake up? When will the masses of Jehovah's witnesses finally rise up and say enough is enough?

The Watchtower society has taken salvation through Jesus away from the Great Crowd. They have given the Great Crowd a home on earth, which is a total lie. They have made the Great Crowd a dead people. They are dead in God's eyes.

Now perhaps you are beginning to see why I had to leave Jehovah's witnesses. They were actually dooming my wife, my family and I to eternal separation from God. I had to make the decision. Would I be wrong with an organization or would I be right with God and the Bible.

That sounds like a dumb question, but that is the statement my father made to me, after I explained to him why I had to leave

Jehovah's witnesses, and before he disowned me. That is also the belief of many of Jehovah's witnesses! If you believe that statement also, then I really have nothing to offer you. Go your lost way and suffer the consequences. But don't say you weren't warned.

However. If you are a lover of truth, now you have a decision to make for you and your family. May God richly bless you as you truly begin to serve the God of the Bible through His precious Son Jesus Christ?

Now, I don't know about you, but I think we could stop right here. This should be enough information to bring us all to our knees asking God to forgive us from our ways of error.

But my friend, there is more. So let's keep going, with the rest of the story!!

# CHAPTER 7

# Where's The Biblical Proof?

Jehovah's witnesses are believers. They believe anything written in the Watchtower publications. They are beautiful people, but they take as gospel whatever the organization of Jehovah's witnesses says.

They have bought the lie, that Jehovah is dispensing His truth on the earth, only through Jehovah's witnesses. Jehovah's witnesses firmly believe that if you are not a Jehovah's witness you are of the devil and will die at the battle of Armageddon.

If you are not a Jehovah's witnesses you are lost. For Jehovah's witnesses it's all about the organization. If the organization says it, they are supposed to do it. In fact when I left the Witnesses I met with 9 elders. I wanted to meet with them and tell them what I had found before I resigned.

I was amazed that they refused to let me share what I found in the Bible that contradicted our beliefs. All the elders were interested in was one question: "Do you believe that the Watchtower organization is Jehovah's sole channel of truth in the world today?"

That's it. Do you believe in the organization!! I would try to talk to them, and they would keep coming back to "Do you believe the organization?" As you can see already, my answer had to be a resounding, NO!! So that leads us to question Number 5 that Jehovah's witnesses cannot answer.

Here it is:

**QUESTION NUMBER 5: Give just one scripture where it specifically says that in the last days, you should look to an organization for the truth?**

Let me quickly answer that for you. There is none!! Jesus said: "I am the way, the truth and the life, no one comes to the father except through me." The Bible says, It's not access to the Father through an organization. It is access to God through Jesus Christ. Jesus Christ is our mediator. Can I make this any plainer?

It is interesting that according to the Watchtower organization, Jesus is not the mediator of the Great Crowd. The organization is the mediator. Isn't that haughty and ridiculous? Well, that was easy. The Witnesses can spend all year looking for a scripture that says, look to an organization. They will not find it. So why do they believe in the organization when the Bible says believe in Jesus?

That is not one of our 20 questions, but it is another good question.

**QUESTION NUMBER 6:** The Watchtower Society says Christ returned invisibly in 1914. Before that they said He returned in 1874. Revelation 1:7 says that when Christ returns, EVERY EYE will see Him. Not a few Watchtower eyes, but EVERY eye shall see Him. **So, the 6ᵗʰ question is: So, If Christ returned in 1914, why didn't EVERY eye see Him?**

This one borders on the absurd. If you can find someone who was alive in 1914, ask them if they saw Christ return in that year. They will think you are crazy. The Bible says that when Christ returns EVERY eye will see Him and Jehovah's witnesses say that when Christ returns, nobody sees Him. Now please. Who are you going to believe? Will you believe the Bible or an organization? End of story!!

Let's leave the absurd and go to the ridiculous. Lets look at question number 7.

**QUESTION NUMBER 7:** To Jehovah's witnesses, "You say that Jehovah is the most important name. You feel it is important that you go door to door telling people about the name of Jehovah. **So question 7 is: Can you give just one scripture where Jesus specifically told His disciples to tell everyone about the name of Jehovah."**

Jehovah's witnesses have this idea of God, that He is sitting up there in heaven, wanting everyone to know His name Jehovah. That's a problem because first of all we really don't know the correct way to pronounce the name Jehovah.

You cannot find the actual name Jehovah in the Old Testament original writings. You can find the consonants YHVH, and then you have to decide what vowels to put in between those consonants. While Jehovah is certainly an accepted form, honestly, we just don't know. God in His wisdom, just never let us really know.

What we do know is not once in the New Testament does Jesus or any of the Apostles in their writings, ever say, *Jehovah is the most important name.* Now let's be reasonable.

If Jehovah's witnesses are right, that Jehovah wants every one to know His name then don't you think that just once, Jesus or His apostles would have said that in the New Testament? No one in the New Testament says Jehovah is the most important name and that God wants everyone to know His name is Jehovah.

Reasonable people in Jehovah's witnesses where are you? How long will you live with the lies of the organization?

Question 8 is basically along the same line as Question 7. Question 7 deals with Jesus telling His disciples about the spreading of the name Jehovah, and Question 8 deals with us. Is there a command for us in the New Testament regarding the name Jehovah.

**So question 8 is: Can you find just one scripture in the New Testament that says you should tell everybody that God's name is Jehovah?**

The answers for 7 and 8 are the same. Nobody in the New Testament says anything about telling the name Jehovah, to anybody. Certainly if it was that important, there should be at least one scripture that says so!! In fact the opposite is true.

Paul says in Philippians chapter 2 verses 9 & 10:

**9. Therefore God has highly exalted Him, and has given Him a <u>name which is above every name</u>, (including Jehovah) 10.**

**That at the name of Jesus every knee should bow, of heavenly ones, and of earthly ones, and of ones under the earth;**

Praise the name of Jesus. It is the most important in the Universe!

# CHAPTER 8

# How About That Jesus

Questions 9 and 10 still deal with the precious name of Jesus. It is such an important topic that we spend quite a few of the 20 questions that Jehovah's witnesses cannot answer on the name of Jesus. The problem with Jehovah's witnesses all comes down to Jesus.

After I left Jehovah's witnesses and became a Christian, my life changed. My attitude became so joyous with the salvation that I had received, that I could hardly believe it. In my younger days, I was a sales manager for a large computerized income tax company. One day I was sitting in my office and this man who worked for me came into my office.

He was one of the more "interesting" people who worked for me. He looked like a hippy. He had long hair and a beard. This guy could have gone to Hollywood and tried out for the part of Jesus in a movie!! He is how I pictured Christ would look.

Anyway, he came into my office, shut my office doors, sat down in front of my desk and said, "I want what you have." So I reached in my pants to give him my money. He started laughing. "No," he said. "I want that joy, that happiness in your life. You are different and I want to be like you." So I led him to the one who always makes a difference in our lives, Jesus.

It's always all about Jesus. And it is Jesus who the Jehovah's witnesses have relegated to a second-class citizen. They want to call themselves Jehovah's Christian witnesses, but they don't have Jesus. They don't really even understand what it means to be "in Christ". They don't really understand what it means to be justified or declared righteous. They really don't understand what it means to be sanctified. They don't understand the wonderful thing that happens to a person when he/she accepts Christ. They give Jesus lip service but they really don't have a clue what it is to be a Christian. Only those who know Jesus as Lord and Savior are really Christians.

When a person really believes in Jesus, a wonderful life begins. 2 Cor. 5:17 says we become a new creature! When we accept Christ, the first thing that happens is our sin is forgiven. Before we accept Christ, we are "dead spiritually". After we accept Christ we become alive spiritually. We are forgiven of our sin and Christ comes to live within us.

Another important thing that happens when we accept Christ, is we become declared righteous, or justified. The Bible says that when we accept Christ, we become God's son.

The Bible says that when we accept Christ, our destination changes. We no longer are citizens of this earth, as our citizenship is in heaven. For the Christian, "to be absent from the body is to be present with the Lord." That means that we no longer fear death. Jesus said, we as Christians never die even though our body gives up.

Look at what He says in John 11:25,26: "I am the resurrection and the life. The one who believes in Me, even if he dies, will live. Everyone who lives and believes in Me will **never die**. Do you believe this?"

What dies is our body. It goes to sleep and there is no knowledge or work in the dead body. That is what Jesus is talking about in verse 25 when He says, "even if he dies."

However in verse 26 when Jesus is talking about those that believe in Him, He says that person will never die. What never dies, when a person dies? It is His spirit!! When a Christian dies, he doesn't die!! He just changes addresses!!

When we die, like Stephen in the book of Acts, chapter 7:59, we can cry out and say: "Lord Jesus receive my spirit". When we who know the Lord die, Jesus receives our spirit and we are alive with Him forever. All of these beliefs, which are scriptural, are out of reach for the Great Crowd. Not because Jesus doesn't want them to have them, but because the Watchtower Society won't let them have them!!

Jehovah's witnesses may say they accept Christ, but none of the above applies to them. If those scriptures don't apply to the Great Crowd, then the Great Crowd remains dead in their sins and are not Christians. Accepting Christ is not a mental, "yes, I believe in Jesus, too", but rather it is giving up your life and your heart to him. It's truly making Him Lord and Savior of your life. The Witnesses talk *about* Jesus, but they really don't let the Great Crowd accept Him.

Their communion celebration corroborates this. Once a year, the Witnesses get together to celebrate communion. Only those who are born again can partake of the cup and the bread. In Witness theology, only the remaining few people of the 144,000 class partake of the emblems. The Great Crowd are passed the cup and the bread but they refuse it. What the Great Crowd is doing by their refusal to drink of the cup, which signifies Christ shed blood as a sacrifice for their sins, is, they are dooming themselves.

They visibly, once a year say NO to the sacrifice of Christ. How horrible. The Great Crowd go on the record each year that they really have not accepted Christ and His redemptive work by the shedding of His blood and the giving of His body for us.

They are the only religion on earth that goes on the record that they reject the sacrifice of Christ every year!! Have you ever heard of such a thing!! Satan is laughing at them!

If the Jehovah's witnesses want to accept Christ they must be born again, as John 3 says. How does that happen? By repenting of your sin and inviting Jesus into your heart. Salvation does not come by works, it comes via a person, and that person is Jesus Christ.

So we have questions 9 and 10 dealing with Jesus. While the New Testament does not say that Jehovah is the most important name, it does say in Philippians 2:9 that JESUS is the most important name.

**So Question 9 is: Why don't you go door to door talking about Jesus instead of Jehovah?**

To my Jehovah's witness audience, you may say you talk about Jesus. But let's be honest. Your message is Jehovah, not Jesus.

**Question 10: In Acts 1:8, Jesus says, "You shall be witnesses of Me" (Jesus). Why aren't you called JESUS WITNESSES instead of Jehovah's witnesses?**

Point: Jehovah's witnesses take their name from Isaiah chapter 43. Every Bible scholar, dead or alive, will tell you that when God said in Isaiah that "You shall be my witnesses", he was talking about the Jews, not some 21<sup>st</sup> century man made organization.

Father open the eyes of those searching. Bless them Father.

# CHAPTER 9

# Lies And Dead People

Jehovah's witnesses are known for their false prophecies. I am not the first to point this out. But Jehovah's witnesses first said that Jesus Christ returned invisibly in 1874 and then they changed that to 1914. That was a pretty important date to change!

Then the Witnesses said that Armageddon was going to happen in 1914, 1915, 1918, 1921, 1925, 1932, 1941 and 1975.

I can remember my father prior to 1975, telling everybody he knew, that the end of the world was going to happen in 1975. Certainly that was the view of many Jehovah's witnesses. Shortly after 1975, over 1 million Jehovah's witnesses left the organization. I feel sorry for the older generation of Witnesses today who really believed that they would never die, but rather would see the battle of Armageddon come and they would live forever on the earth. Now so many older Jehovah's witnesses are in the final years of their lives without ever seeing the false promise that the Watchtower Society gave them. It is sad to see. I have to believe that in the quiet of their own rooms at night, many of them have to be wondering if they made the right decision in joining Jehovah's witnesses. Unfortunately the answer to that question is that they made the wrong decision! But its not too late for them, if they would believe on the Lord Jesus!

Because of all of their false promises and false prophecies, all the Watchtower Bible and Tract Society will say now about the end of the world, is that it is going to happen soon. The end of the world coming soon has always been a motivating force in bringing people into the organization. But really the Watchtower Bible and Tract Society is a false prophet!! That alone should be enough to wake up Jehovah's witnesses.

I mean if someone lied to me at least 7 times about any subject, I would no longer follow them.

**So here is question number 11:**

**The Watchtower Society predicted the end of the world would come in 1914, 1915, 1918, 1921, 1925, 1932, 1941 and 1975. They lied. So the question is: Who is the father of the lie?**

The answer to that question is profound. The father of the lie, obviously is Satan. If Jehovah's witnesses call their organization, "THE TRUTH", isn't it strange that they would follow a satanic lie!

Now we know that Jehovah's witnesses believe there are two classes of people in their organization, the 144,000 and the Great Crowd.

In Romans Chapter 8, we find that there is one class, called "of the Spirit" and there is another class called "of the Flesh". Paul says that those of the Spirit live and those of the flesh die.

In Jehovah's witnesses theology those of the Spirit are only those of the 144,000 class. The Great Crowd are not of the Spirit and are not of that class. If that is the case, then that means that those of the Great Crowd are of the flesh.

So, in light of what we have discussed about Romans 8, here is question 12.

**QUESTION 12:** There are two classes of people mentioned in Romans Chapter 8. There are those of the Spirit, which Jw's say are members of the 144,000 and those of the flesh. Romans 8 says those of the Spirit have life and those of the flesh die. If you are a member of the Great Crowd, you must be of the flesh because you are not of the Spirit.

**So Question 12 is: If you are of the flesh and the Bible says those of the flesh die, what kind of a hope for the future is that?**

**That then leads to question 13.** Taking question 12 one step further, Romans 8:1-10 shows that if you do not have Christ and if you are not of the Spirit, then you are condemned.

**So Question 13 is: How can you gain life in God's New Order if you are Condemned?**

Lord Jesus, help us to see your grace and mercy. Bring all truth seekers into your family!! Especially bless those older Witnesses who have been mislead. Lead them to you Jesus!

Let's move on. Seven more questions to go!

# CHAPTER 10

# Where's The Hope?

Years ago, there was a funny television commercial that asked the question, "Where's the Beef". I can modify that question a little and ask when it comes to Jehovah's witnesses,, "Where's the hope"?

What most Jehovah's witnesses and all those other good people on earth who don't have Christ don't understand is that before we meet Jesus, the Bible speaks of us as dead in our sins. We are really dead spiritually.

Remember when God told Adam that in the day that they would eat of the fruit of the tree of the knowledge of good and evil that they would die? Many wonder why after they ate of the fruit they didn't just drop dead. In fact they lived on and Adam physically died, at the age of 930 years.

So whats the deal. Was God lying when He told Adam he would die in the day he ate the fruit? No. Adam did die the day he ate the fruit. He died spiritually. By the way, everyone wants to know what kind of a fruit it was that Adam ate. It must have been a pear, because Adam ate the fruit and lost his Pear-adise!! Forgive me!!

Anyway, the scriptures tell us that all of us inherited that same spiritually dead condition at birth. It is only when we accept Jesus Christ as our Lord and Savior, that we become alive. That's not me talking, that's the Bible talking. Let's look and see.

Eph 2:1 And **you were dead** in your trespasses and sins

Eph 2:2 in which you previously walked according to this worldly age, according to the ruler of the atmospheric domain, the spirit now working in the disobedient.

Eph 2:3 We too all previously lived among them in our fleshly desires, carrying out the inclinations of our flesh and thoughts, and by nature we were children under wrath, as the others were also.

Eph 2:4 But God, who is abundant in mercy, because of His great love that He had for us,

Eph 2:5 made **us alive** with the Messiah even though **we were dead in trespasses**. By grace you are saved!

Eph 2:6 He also raised us up with Him and seated us with Him in the heavens, in Christ Jesus,

Eph 2:7 so that in the coming ages He might display the immeasurable riches of His grace in *His* kindness to us in Christ Jesus.

Eph 2:8 For by grace you are saved through faith, and this is not from yourselves; it is God's gift—

Eph 2:9 not from works, so that no one can boast.

Eph 2:10 For we are His creation—created in Christ Jesus for good works, which God prepared ahead of time so that we should walk in them.

God's word tells us that no amount of works can establish a relationship with God and make us alive. It is a spiritual problem. So God solved the problem. He sent His Son to die for our sins, and thus give us life. Praise the Lord!!

Now Jehovah's witnesses do not understand that concept, because they also believe that there is no spirit that lives on. They still follow the false Adventist doctrine! They believe that the spirit is basically their breath. God breathed into Adam His breath and that is what the spirit is according to the Witnesses.

What Jehovah's witnesses miss is that when God breathed into Adam, He gave Adam a life giving spirit. Adam had a spirit and it was alive. Paul said to be *absent from the body is to be present with the Lord*. If the spirit doesn't live on, then what does that mean. What goes to heaven to be present with the Lord?

Stephen said in Acts when about to die, "Lord Jesus, receive my spirit". If the spirit doesn't live on, then what did Stephen mean when he said that? What was Jesus to receive of Stephen? Was Jesus just going to catch his breath!!

So what we want to see happen in our lives, is for our spirit to be alive. Think of the possiblities when our spirit is alive. The Bible says we commune with God. Romans 8:16 says that God's Spirit bears witness with our spirit that we are sons of God.

When your spirit is alive, the Holy Spirit deals with you as God's child. He nudges you, He convicts you, He encourages you, He teaches you and He molds you and conforms you to the image Jesus. That is what Romans 8:29 is all about. Its says: "For those He foreknew He also predestined to be conformed to the image of His Son, so that He would be the firstborn among many brothers."

So, believing in Jesus is not just a statement. It is not just a way of belief. Many times, you will hear a Jehovah's witness say, "oh, we believe in Jesus." Jehovah's witnesses believe in Jesus, just like Satan believes in Jesus. They know He is there, but they don't accept Him as a personal Savior. Remember also, that when a Witnesses says "I believe in Jesus" they are really saying, I believe that Jesus is Michael the Archangel!!

Now, in considering salvation, if you are a Witness, in what way are you different than a non Jehovah's witness. Think about it. A non-Jehovah's witness doesn't know Jesus and you don't know Jesus. You are both dead in God's eyes, regardless of how good you are and how hard you work. God doesn't let just "good people" into His family!!

There is only one way of salvation and there is only one way to not be dead in God's eyes. That way is Jesus. He is the way the truth and the life!! "All who believe on Jesus will be saved". So the next four questions of the 20 questions Jehovah's witnesses cannot answer deal with this subject.

**QUESTION 14:** The Watchtower Society says that members of the Great Crowd, are those people spoken of in Revelation 20:5, where it says: "the rest of the dead do not come to life until the thousand years has ended." They, your Watchtower and Bible and Tract Society, says, you are the *dead in God's eyes.*

**So Question14 is***: If you are a member of the Great Crowd,* **How does it feel for you and your family to be dead in God's eyes?**

The next question is related and it also deals with the "death" subject.

**QUESTION 15:** Ephesians 2:1 says that before we accept Christ as our Lord that we are ALL <u>dead in our trespasses.</u>

**So Question 15 is: As a member of the Great Crowd who wants to live on the earth, how do you ever get over your being dead in your trespasses and dead in God's eyes?**

That is a great question with sobering consequences to its answer.

Let's look now at the next question. I have talked about it before as part of my testimony in leaving the Witnesses. Now let's look at it from the stand point as a powerful question that Jehovah's witnesses cannot answer.

**QUESTION 16:** The Watchtower Society says you are not a Son of God. Only those of the 144,000 are.

Do you pray for God's Spirit to lead you? Romans 8:14 says, "All who are led by God's Spirit are sons of God." <u>All means ALL</u>!

If you pray for, and expect God's Spirit to lead you, then, Romans 8 says you are a Son of God. That is what the Bible says. The Watchtower Society says no. They say you can pray for the Spirit to lead you, but you are not a son of God.

**So Question 16 is:** *Who do you believe? The Bible or the Watchtower Society?*

What is sad, is most of the Great Crowd will believe the Watchtower organization over what the Bible says!

**QUESTION 17: Why do you let the Watchtower Society keep you dead in God's eyes instead of alive in Christ and filled with His Spirit?**

Ask yourself: What about this religion of Jehovah's witnesses attracts you to them? You are spiritually dead. It is uncanny, but when you come down to it, on this point, The Witnesses are right. The Great Crowd in their present state, are dead in God's eyes.

I remember what it was like being a Jehovah's witness. I was empty. I was going through the motions. I went to every meeting. I prepared my talks with diligence. I faithfully knocked on doors with the Watchtower publications. I served as an elder. I went to the committee meetings. I spoke at conventions. I sang their songs. I was what I thought a good person. But I was empty.

I knew something was missing in my life. I had a great wife, 3 beautiful children, a great secular job, drove new cars, and lived in a paradise climate. But I was running on empty.

Now listen to me. Do I have your attention? If you are a

Jehovah's witness reading this book, and if you are honest, you are running on empty. There is a void in your heart. You know something is wrong, but you don't know what it is.

I will tell you what it is. You need Jesus to come into your life and fill that void.

You can do that right now. Pray with me: "Lord Jesus, I am sorry for all the years I have ignored you. Lord I confess today that I am a sinner. I repent of that sin Lord. Forgive me of my sins Lord. I accept you as my Lord and as my Savior. Come into my life Lord. Make me alive in you. Cover me with your righteousness. I love you Lord. In Jesus name, Amen."

My friend, its not just the words. There is no magic in the words. But if you said that prayer and truly mean it from the bottom of your heart, you now know Jesus Christ as Lord and Savior.

Welcome to the family of God. Now when God looks at you He says: "That's my boy. That's my girl!" Praise be to the Lord!! YOU ARE ALIVE!!

# CHAPTER 11

# Let's Talk Resurrection

Jehovah's witnesses have been taught a really big lie when it comes to the resurrection. I mentioned this as I began this book.

While it is interesting that the 144,000 must have a spirit according to Jehovah's witnesses, because when they die, they go directly to heaven. The Great Crowd when they die, they just go out of existance. What is amazing to me is that the Great Crowd really considers that a "great hope".

Let me see if I have this right. When I die as a member of the Great Crowd, I go out of existance. And that's a hope? I don't think so. Now so you don't get the wrong idea, I want you to understand that if you talk to a Jehovah's witness, they will tell you they believe in the resurrection.

But is it really resurrection they believe in? Like most doctrines of Jehovah's witnesses, the average Jehovah's witness has not thought it through. Here is what Jehovah's witnesses teach happens to the Great Crowd when they die. They go out of existance. The body goes to the grave and poof, they are out of existance. Now their hope is that during the thousand years spoken of in the book of Revelation that God will bring them back to life.

The first problem is, there is absolutely no scripture that specifically says that. So they pin their whole hope of resurrection on a "teaching of the Watchtower Society" and not on the facts of the Bible.

Now let's look at their "resurrection". Remember, when the Great Crowd die according to their belief, they go out of existance. So their hope is that in the new world, God will make a new body for them, and put into them the memories they had when they lived on the earth.

That is not resurrection. That is some kind of recreation. As I mentioned in my testimony, it is taking a body, somebody elses body, and putting my memory in it. It could be likened to, building a robot, and in its memory banks, I would put my memory. Try as you want, that is not me. It is another body with my memories. That is not hope for me. That is spookie!!

Now let me tell you what the real resurrection is. When we who know Christ die, our body goes into the grave, where there is no more wisdom or knowledge or speaking or thinking. But our spirit which is alive, goes to be with the Lord. That is why Paul could say those words we have heard before in this book: "To be absent in the body is to be present with the Lord."

Then when Christ returns, 1 Thessalonians 4:13-18 says that God brings with Him those who have physically died. What does God bring with Him when Jesus returns? The spirits of all who have died.

When Christ returns, He brings with Him those of us who have died before He returned. At that time, He gathers up all of the saints left on the earth, and catches them up into the sky and He gives us all, those who died throughout the ages, and we who are caught up to meet the Lord in the air, our resurrection bodies. We all receive our resurrection body at the same time!

1 Corinthians 15 says that we shall be changed in the twinkling of an eye. It says that this which is mortal (our body) must put on immortality, (our resurrection body). What a hope!! Our spirit lives on after we die. We go directly to live with the Lord. Then at some-time in the future, when Christ returns, He gives us our resurrection body, with our living spirit in it and forever we live with the Lord!!

Now that is what the Bible says. We are not making it up. Check it out for yourselves. Christians have a living hope. That is why Jesus said, that we would never die, even though our body went to sleep. Friends that is hope.

So the next question of the 20 questions Jehovah's witnesses cannot answer deals with the subject of resurrection. These are very important questions because they are about your future, so listen up!!

QUESTION 18: If you are a member of the Great Crowd, The Watchtower Society teaches you that should you die now, you will be resurrected **during** the thousand years.

**So Question 18 is: Can you quote just one Scripture that specifically says that should you die before Armageddon that you would be resurrected during the thousand years?**

At some point in time you have to ask yourselves, "do I trust this organization who teaches and believes differently than what the Bible says, with my life and the life of my family." This may surprise you, but there is no scripture that says *the Great Crowd will live on earth.* There is no scripture that says the *Great Crowd will be resurrected during the thousand years.* Those are just "positions" taken by the Watchtower Society and created by, you guessed it, our boozing buddy, old, dead, Judge Rutherford.

According to Watchtower doctrine the Great Crowd, or more personally **you**, are dead in God's eyes, not of the spirit and **you are condemned by God.** Are you willing to gamble your life, based upon beliefs not found in the Bible? It makes no sense!!

Let me challenge you. Take your Bible and try to prove the Watchtower Society right.

When they say something in their publications and lay down a scriptural text in the copy, read the scripture they have given as a source of their belief. Make sure the scriptures say specifically what the Society says they say. You will be amazed how terrible their theology is.

Jehovah's witnesses use scriptures to back up their message that are totally out of context and don't even apply.

As I started looking more closely at how the Jehovah's witnesses did things in their publications, I made a very troubling discovery.

In their Watchtower that they study faithfully, you will find statements made and then scripture references laid next to the point they are making. When you look up the scripture, you find that either the reference has nothing to do with the statement made, or you find that the scripture was totally quoted out of context.

Let me also make this comment about the Jehovah's witness Bible. All scholars I know make a point about the New World Translation and how bad it is. It certainly leaves a lot to be desired.

And yes, there are things there that are not in the original texts. But I must confess, I met Jesus reading the New World Translation!! So even as bad as that translation may be, the gospel can still be found.

Please, read the Bible carefully. It is important. Your life, and the life of your family are at risk.

# CHAPTER 12

# How About That Gospel!!

Jehovah's witnesses love to talk about Mathew 24:14. "This good news of the kingdom shall be preached in all the earth for a witness and then the end will come."

I called on over 30,000 homes as a Jehovah's witnesses. Many times I quoted that scripture.

Of course Jehovah's witnesses think they have the gospel. They preach all over the world that Jehovah has establish His kingdom in the heavens in 1914, when Jesus invisibly returned and that He is working through Jehovah's witnesses on the earth to spread His message that His name is Jehovah.

Jehovah's witnesses teach that soon Armageddon will come to destroy all bad people who are not Jehovah's witnesses. According to Jehovah's witnesses the way you gain salvation is to work.

We know the gospel is not one of works because Ephesians 2:8,9 says we are saved by grace through faith, not of works. If we were saved by works we could boast!! Throughout eternity we could say, "Look at me. I did it! I earned my salvation!!"

The gospel is incredibly simple. Even a child can understand it without the help of an organization. The gospel is straightforward. Salvation is not accomplished by something we do. Salvation is accomplished by putting faith in the One who already did all the work. Remember, Jesus said: "It is finished". No more work to do. All we need to do is believe. That's it. We must put faith in Jesus Christ. Now for many that is too simple. But that's it.

If what we needed to be saved from our sin was an education, God would have sent us an educator. If what we needed to be saved from our death sentenced was to learn how to speak well and go door to door, God would have sent us a salesman. But our problem was sin. *For all have sinned and fall short of the glory of God.* What we needed to be saved from death was someone to carry our sin. We needed a Savior.

That is why our Heavenly Father supplied His only begotten Son, to come to this earth and die for our sins, and to be resurrected on the third day.

So, in harmony with that, we have question number 19.

**QUESTION 19:** 1 Corinthians 15:3,4 specifically tells us what the Gospel is: Christ died, was buried and then resurrected. That is not the gospel of Jehovah's witnesses. Instead they preach the gospel as, Christ returned invisibly in 1914. That is a different gospel than what Paul taught. There is no record anywhere in the Bible where Paul taught to watch for a new gospel to arrive on the scene that said, Christ would return in 1914!! In fact, Galatians 1:8 says that *anyone* who preached a different gospel than the one he taught in 1 Corinthians 15:1-4, would be accursed.

**So Question 19 is: You teach a different gospel than what is found in the New Testament. Doesn't that make you accursed?**

I must tell you how amazed I was that salvation was by faith instead of by works. One of the Witnesses favorite scriptures is in James when he says: "Faith without works is dead". They use that to try and prove you have to work. That scriputre doesn't address that issue at all. James is telling us how we know we have put faith in Jesus. Works is an outcome of our faith, not the thing that gives us faith. Let me tell you a little secret. I know what I am talking about when it comes to works. I wanted to do my salvation for myself and by myself. When I found out that the job had already been done by the sacrifice of our Lord Jesus and all that I could do was believe, all I could say was: PRAISE THE NAME OF JESUS. Now as a Jehovah's witness I was never convinced that if Armaggedon was to come that I would make it through. I hoped I would, but I never knew if I was going to be good enough to make it.

What if I had skipped a couple of meetings the month before Armaggedon. What if I didn't go out in service enough hours the month before, would I make it. What if I didn't study the Watchtower for a month or so? If Armaggedon was to come would I make it? What if I lusted after a pretty girl for 3 seconds? What if I happened to have a little too much wine one day. You see, that is the trouble with "works" religion. You can never be sure that you have done all you could do to merit your salvation.

Jehovah's witnesses know nothing of any assurance of salvation. They just always hope that they have been good enough.

So that brings us to the final question.

**QUESTION 20:** 1 John 5:13 says, that you **may know** that you have eternal life. When you believe in Jesus as your Lord and Savior, He gives you the assurance that you have life. The Watchtower Society would have you believe that you can *only hope* you make it into the New Order.

**So question 20 is:** *1 John 5:13 says you may know you have eternal life. Why don't you know it?*

**Point:** Jesus Loves you. He died for you. Romans 3:23 says you are a condemned sinner, but Romans 6:23 says God forgives that sin through Jesus Christ.

Acts 16:31 says "believe on the Lord Jesus Christ and be saved." You are not saved by being good or working hard. It is impossible to work that hard or be that good!! You are saved by a free gift and that free gift is Jesus Christ.

John 3:16 says that Jesus died personally, <u>for you</u>. Won't you ask Jesus into your heart today. Begin the new Spirit filled life.

**God has something great for you. His name is Jesus!!** May you and your family enjoy the future with Jesus!!

Father you are so awesome. May the readers of this book be blessed!!

# CHAPTER 13

# The Big Problem

There is a real problem at the headquarters of Jehovah's witnesses. There may not be enough Jehovah's witnesses who truly understand their doctrine the way they should, but this problem is big enough to ruin their religion.

Let me explain.

Jehovah's witnesses believe that around 1918 after Jesus had come invisibly in 1914, that Jehovah looked around at all the religions in the world. He saw that they were all wrong, except for Jehovah's witnesses. It was around that time in 1918 that Jehovah determined that there was one group of people that did have the truth. It was, you guessed it, the group that would be called Jehovah's witnesses.

So according to the Witnesses, Jehovah decided to work through their organization. He decided that He would work through the anointed class, (the 144,000) and that through this group, who they called the *faithful and discreet slave*, in harmony with

Matthew chapter 25, Jehovah would dispense His food to everyone else in the world.

According to their belief, and this has been central to their doctrine all these years, Jehovah would not work with anyone else but the anointed or those of the 144,000 class. This is a core doctrine of Jehovah's witnesses. No faithful and discreet slave class, no dispensing of spiritual food coming from Jehovah. That is why we all had to obey the organization, because the anointed where getting spiritual food from Jehovah and passing it along through their publications, like the Watchtower.

Now in practical application, at first the term "anointed" basically referred to the President of the Watchtower society.

So in the 1920's, 30's and until his death in the early 40's, that meant that Jehovah was dispensing His food through one of the anointed, the second president of the Watchtower society, old gin breath, Judge Rutherford.

In the 40's, 50's 60's and 70's, that began to broaden out a little. Brother Knorr and Brother Franz were basically the people with the final say on things written in the publications. But they were still of the anointed. (Remember Jehovah's witnesses believe that only members of the 144,000 are of the anointed.)

Later in the 80's and 90's as Knorr and Franz died off, power was turned over to a group of the anointed. They were called the governing body. These were basically old time Jehovah's witnesses who had been with the organization for years. In order to be on the governing body, you had to be of the anointed. That made you a member of the faithful and discreet slave class who was in charge of dispensing the word of God to the masses, the Great Crowd. At first there were 18 or so who were members of the governing body.

But something happened.

Jehovah's witnesses never expected Armageddon not to come. They failed to plan on one small thing. If Jehovah didn't bring on Armageddon for say, 50 years, all of the anointed would be dead (because remember they stopped picking them in 1935).

Well it has now been more than 70 years since the last members of the anointed were selected and no Armageddon.

Now the remaining members of the Governing Body of the Watchtower Society are so old that they must retire or step aside. That means that the only people left to be in charge are members of the Great Crowd, the non-anointed!! That has many ramifications which the Witnesses have not yet figured out. Because the Great Crowd are not anointed, that means that they cannot feed the sheep, because THEY ARE the sheep!

Remember, according to Jehovah's witnesses own doctrine, God looked around and found no religion that had it right, so He chose the anointed, the 144,000 class of Jehovah's witnesses to be the faithful and discreet slave. According to the Witnesses Jehovah would only work through the Spirit led anointed class. It was only the anointed class that could dispense spiritual food to the Great Crowd. Now that the anointed are almost all gone or too old to function in the capacity as leaders, Jehovah's witnesses have an organization being run by non-anointed Jehovah's witnesses. That can't be. That can't work! It goes against the whole basis of Jehovah's witnesses doctrine.

If there are no anointed left, how can Jehovah's witnesses be so blind and bold to say that they are the only ones who have the truth, when their organization is now being run by ordinary members of the Great Crowd, who have no anointing and are not chosen by

Jehovah to run the show!!

According to Jehovah's witnesses own theology, the Great Crowd do not have the Holy Spirit and have **no commission** to run the headquarters of Jehovah's witnesses because they are just members of the Great Crowd. Since when do sheep lead sheep!! Sheep don't feed the Sheep!!

This false doctrine that the Great Crowd do not have the Holy Spirit and anointing from God will cause much trouble for thinking Jehovah's witnesses. To have the Great Crowd in charge of the Watchtower Bible and Tract Society goes against everything Jehovah's witnesses have taught over the past 100 years. I pray and expect to see something happen in the future that will cause a great awakening among honest hearted Jehovah's witnesses. Please pray for that.

# CHAPTER 14

# I Found Jesus

I had been a happy Jehovah's witness for 30 years. Then after reading the New World Translation's New Testament 9 times, I came to understand that the whole of Jehovah's witnesses doctrine was based on shifting sand. Scripture did not prove their beliefs. In fact, scripture disproved each and every one of their important doctrines.

After doing much studying and reading I knew in my mind what I had to do. I knew I had to invite Jesus into my life and heart. The problem was, I was afraid. I was afraid it just couldn't be that simple. So I held back. I just couldn't believe on Jesus for salvation, even though in my mind I knew that is what I had to do.

One Saturday morning, I was meeting for field service. (That's what we called the door to door work. We always met together as a group for a few minutes before going out and knocking on doors.) This particular morning we were meeting at one of the ministerial servants homes. A ministerial servant was the equivalency of a deacon in the church. His name was Jim and after we had said a prayer in preparation to take the Witness gospel to the people, Jim pulled me aside and said he wanted to talk to me.

I followed Jim into his kitchen and listened intently as he said to me: "Chuck, I am going to tell you something that will knock your socks off. You are not going to believe what I am going to tell you but I think that the 144,000 number is not a literal number. I think the Witnesses have it all wrong." I couldn't believe what I was hearing. One of my friends, was having thoughts about some of the same things I had be researching!

So I told Jim to bring his wife over to my house that night and we could play some cards together and maybe talk about that issue. You must remember that up until this time, Deanna and I were studying, but I was the presiding overseer in the congregation I was in and I had said nothing to anyone in the congregation about what I had been finding.

That night Jim and his wife came to our house. After a while of playing cards we stopped and spent a little time talking about what Jim had said to me that morning. I didn't know how committed Jim was to finding the real truth, so I didn't go into much detail as to what I was finding in my studies.

As we concluded the night, I asked Jim and his wife to go home and read the book of Romans. I asked them to come back the following Saturday night and I told them that if they found something interesting we would talk, and if they didn't find anything interesting we would have a good time playing cards. Well, the next Saturday came and Jim and his wife Tania came to our home. I will remember this until the day I die.

I asked them both if they had a chance to read the book of

Romans. Tania was sitting on the sofa and she began to cry. She looked at me and said: "We who accept Christ as Lord and Savior are all going to go to heaven!!" Talk about an exciting night. Now I knew I could share everything I had learned with people who had the light go on! They got it! The Lord had opened their eyes, and they were on the way to salvation!

Soon after this, Jim and Tania explained the truth to her parents who also were Jehovah's witnesses. They jumped at the chance to learn the real truth! Her parents then shared the truth with some of their Witness friends. Eventually we had about 40 people in the congregation who began a journey for the real truth. We began two Bible studies a week to search the Bible so that we could really understand what Christianity was all about.

On Wednesday nights we would read the New Testament together. When we found something that stood out, we would talk about it. On Sunday mornings, Jim or I would take a doctrine of Jehovah's witnesses and try to prove them RIGHT. The group also had input in this study. I must admit that this was one the richest times of learning in my whole life. Truly the Holy Spirit was there teaching us. We would go into the meetings with some of our own ideas, and the Holy Spirit would show us how we were either right or wrong. It was amazing how the Holy Spirit directed!

It was at the beginning of these Bible studies that I had to take a trip to Dallas for the company I was working for. Even though we had a great study plan going, I didn't know the Lord yet and I was still somewhat confused. I knew in my mind what I had to do, but it just sounded so simple!!

I got to Dallas, and as I got off the plane, the first thing that happens is that I run into the "Moonies" at the airport. They tried to get me to take their books.

I got to my hotel and just as I got to the lobby I ran into a couple of Mormon boys who gave me a Mormon bible. As I got into the elevator, I noticed that there were noisy black ladies filling the elevator. They told me they were Christians, visiting Dallas for a Black Gospel convention!! All I heard in the elevator was Praise the Lord, Praise the Lord! I thought to myself, these women are "Wacky!"

I didn't understand that soon I would be "Wacky" too!! Looking back on that elevator experience I have much joy over that beautiful time. These women were so much in love with Jesus that it radiated! What a witness for Jesus they were!!

When I got into my room, I found that I had a message on my phone. The message was from a member of the Dawn, a splinter group of Jehovah's witnesses. The man who ran the show in Dallas had somehow heard I was coming to town and he wanted to talk to me. He came to my hotel and we spent a couple of hours together, talking about false Witness doctrine. Unlike the Black women in the elevator, this guy was just plain boring!!

After this Dawnite left, I was really confused. I had met all of these religious people this day. What was God trying to show me? I decided I needed a change of scenery, so I thought it might be good for me to clear my head and go to the movies. There was only one problem. I didn't know where there was a theater. I got into my rented car and I decided to drive around and find one.

It wasn't long that I approached a small shopping center. I could see some marquee lights. I knew there was a theatre there. I was anxious to see what movie was showing. To my amazement, as I drove up to the theater I saw what was playing. It was a movie called BORN AGAIN. It was a movie about the life of Chuck Colson, and his struggle that led to his belief in Jesus.

Talk about a God moment!! I couldn't believe it. Naturally, I decided to go and see the show.

As I watched the movie, I saw myself in Chuck Colson. His doubts were the same doubts that I had. He had a head knowledge of Jesus, but he just couldn't give it up. He couldn't accept Christ as his Lord and Savior. It was too simple. It was too easy.

About half way through the movie, Colson accepts Christ. It was at that point that Jesus touched my heart. It was years later that I personally met Chuck Colson and shared with him what his movie did to my life!! As I watched Colson accept Christ, I started crying and I had to leave the theater. I got out in the car and sat there three hours basking in the love of Jesus.

It was there in the car in the parking lot of a movie theater in Dallas, Texas, on a warm October evening that I met Jesus Christ as my Lord and Savior. I haven't been the same since. At that moment in Dallas, I became a new creature in Jesus, filled with the Holy Spirit, declared righteous, an Heir with Christ, a child of God, with my sins forgiven.

**I WAS BORN AGAIN!!**

I called my wife Deanna and told her what happened. I came back to California and told the group of 40 what happened. Soon, all 40 people in our Bible study became Born Again. How God blessed us!! Jesus came into all of our lives and we knew we were all going to spend an eternity with our risen Savior, in heaven.

The journey was worth it. The loss of our friends was worth it. My father calling me and disowning me was worth it. We basically gave it all up for Jesus, and I must tell you He is trustworthy. There is nothing like living in Christ!!

Jesus Christ took a young man and young woman who spent the first 30 years of their life as Jehovah's witnesses and brought them into His family. What a privilege! I must tell you a secret!! I'm so glad I know Jesus.

It is my prayer that you will too!

# CHAPTER 15

# There IS Life
# After Jehovah's witnesses

It has been several decades now since my wife and I left Jehovah's witnesses

Life has been good. I once was young but now I am old, entering into the last decades of my life.

At the writing of this book, Deanna and I have been married 40 years and have 3 adult children with 9 beautiful grandchildren. We have the addition to our family of one beautiful daughter-in-law and two handsome son-in-laws! We are truly blessed.

My three children, on their own, have accepted Jesus Christ as their Lord and Savior. Our children's spouses have all met the Lord.

I am so proud of my children. They are great people who are all involved in ministry in one form or another. They are such a blessing to me. They have made this journey well worth it.

At the writing of this book, my nine grandchildren are all under 8 years old, but the two oldest, Trevor and Tori have also accepted

Christ. What a blessing!! It is our prayer that the other magnificent 7 will follow in their footsteps. We know and trust that they will! They are my entire legacy!! One of my younger grandsons, Austin, I believe is destined to be the next Billy Graham!!

Deanna and I live comfortably in a resort community in California. At the writing of this book, I am the senior pastor of a church called Cornerstone, but I am soon to retire to writing and training pastors for ministry, in a seminary I have been privileged to establish.

While we lost almost all of our friends when we left the Witnesses which has pained us throughout the years, we have gained hundreds more of true friends who have replaced them. God has blessed us with more true friends than we can count. They are so precious to us!! Praise the Lord!! We are all in the same family and we will all live for an eternity together.

We are financially taken care of and spiritually alive and active.

I have so many experiences to tell that it would fill many more volumes. Lord willing, I have many more books to write.

One blessing that I have not previously mentioned in this book is that my youngest brother has become a Christian. I thank the Lord for His Grace and Mercy!!

My father who disowned me after I became a Christian remained a Witness until his death. I am sad to say that it appears that he died without knowing Jesus Christ.

At the time of my writing this book, my mother is still alive. She is still a Jehovah's witness. I pray she will come to know the real Jesus before it is too late.

I had another brother who had cerebral palsy. His name is Johnny. Johnny died a few years ago. But I must tell you something wonderful. Before he died, Johnny accepted Jesus Christ as Lord and Savior. I was privileged to lead him to the Lord.

If you ever attend one of my seminars, you will hear the story of Johnny's coming to Jesus. It is the most awesome experience I have ever had. When you hear it, it will bring you to tears and will motivate you to share Jesus with all you know. Johnny could not talk and it was very difficult to know if he truly had accepted Christ. But Jesus did something through Johnny that left absolutely no doubt. I know for a 100% certainty that when I get to heaven, I will see Johnny there. I have never told my mother about Johnny. Perhaps before she dies I will.

I want to close with a letter I received from my daughter, Heather, on our 40th wedding anniversary. I was especially touched by the last paragraph.

Heather was 7 when we left the Witnesses yet she understands that what we did many years ago, saved her and her children's lives. She blessed me with this letter.

Dear Mom and Dear Dad,

Wow, where do I begin? You are both such an inspiration to us all and we wish we could do so much more for you at this time because to be married for 40 years is such a huge accomplishment. Time is going so fast, especially now as we are all having children of our own, that we often do not take time to let the ones we know how much we love and admire them so I am glad for times like these.

Mom, I love you so much. You taught me so much and even though we do not like the same foods, I know I am of your mold. You are the best mom in the whole world and I know that sounds like something a five year old would write but I really mean it. I mean I really get it now. Now that I have my own children, I see you in such a different light. Everything I go through with my children, I know you had to do with me and my brother and sister............So with a large amount of gratitude, I thank you, for everything, from the smallest little gestures to always being there for me.

Dad, I love you so much. You always gave me the confidence to do anything I put my mind to. You made me strong and I have always felt so happy and content with myself as a person and I truly believe that a lot of women grow up in this world without that. I can only hope I can give this same gift to my children. I am very lucky that I have a father who I know is very proud of me. A long time ago, you wrote me a letter at Christmas time that you probably forgot about but I keep it in my Bible and read it often and it tells me of all of those things that I just talked about. You truly are a great daddy and I love you!

And last but not least. To both of you. I thank you for bringing me to know the Lord. Today I have a personal relationship with Him and I know that would not be the case if you would had not done what you did, so many years ago. I know it was a difficult thing for you to do in leaving Jehovah's witnesses, but now you have a legacy of children and grandchildren that will grow up knowing the Lord. I hope you both have the happiest 40<sup>th</sup> Anniversary.

Love, Heather

My friends, that is what it is all about. Family.

God wants you to become a member of His family and He does that by offering you His son Jesus. I trust you will believe in Jesus, today, if you don't already know Him.

Thank you for reading this book.

It is my hope that you will use it as your tool to help those who either are Jehovah's witnesses or who are studying with them or are beginning to explore their religion.

Give them a copy of this book. Pray for them. Let the Lord work in their lives. Honest hearted people who read this book, will soon see the real truth.

If you are currently a Jehovah's witness and If you are in need of help with your walk away from the Witnesses, or you have any questions or comments, please visit our web site and send me an email.

Our Web Site is: www.Love4jws.com. You will find my current e-mail contact on that site or you will find a way to e-mail me. I would love to hear from you. I promise to keep your information confidential.

We have also made the **20 questions that Jehovah's witnesses cannot answer** into a tract that might be helpful in your ministry. You can get those on our website.

I also have 2 videos that I made years ago that might be interesting for you. You can order them on the website www.love4jws.com. Just remember one thing. I made those videos when I was young and good-looking!! I have changed a bit throughout the years!!

I pray this book has been a blessing to you.

There **IS** life after Jehovah's witnesses. It is a great, fulfilled life. I am a testimony to that fact!!

May God richly bless you as you walk with His glorious Son, Jesus.

Printed in the United States
84670LV00009B/166/A